Idle Thoughts...

By
Peter Lancaster

(After Jerome K. Jerome)

An environmentally friendly book printed and bound in England by
www.printondemand-worldwide.com

Idle Thoughts

I know there are mischievous fairies,
Locked up tight inside my head,
Breaking out when I am sleeping,
Clamour-clawing to be fed.

They frisk and frolic through my brain,
Like tracers in the dark,
Whispering their fairy tales,
Which often miss the mark.

The naughty secrets in their laughter,
Itch my eyelids open wide,
But in the blackness they have vanished,
Scattering to run and hide.

Still I know that they are sending,
Thoughts like dandelion seeds,
Germinating in the mind's eye,
Sometimes flowers,
Sometimes weeds.

http://www.fast-print.net/bookshop

IDLE THOUGHTS
Copyright © Peter Lanacster 2016

All rights reserved

No part of this book may be reproduced in any form by photocopying or any electronic or mechanical means, including information storage or retrieval systems, without permission in writing from both the copyright owner and the publisher of the book.

All characters are fictional.
Any similarity to any actual person is purely coincidental.

The right of Peter Lancaster to be identified as the author of this work has been asserted by him in accordance with the Copyright, Designs and Patents Act 1988 and any subsequent amendments thereto.

A catalogue record for this book is available from the British Library

ISBN 978-178456-344-8

First published 2016 by
FASTPRINT PUBLISHING
Peterborough, England.

For my grandson, Jack

A note of thanks...

Thanks to the wonderful illustrator David Ball who has added another dimension to this book with his brilliant, dysfunctional fairies.

Thanks to Mike Hawthorne, Chris Kirwan, Roy Standring and David Baker for their encouragement and advice.

Thanks to Roy Chng for his technical wizardry in transposing the pictures.

To quote Ringo Starr, 'Peace and love, peace and love'.

List of Illustrations

Clock That	ii
Satnav	25
Dragonweld	31
Web-Mistress	37
Think Pink	39
Snapdragon	57
Moon Daisy	67
Hi!	71
Petal	77
Power Play	81
Who nicked all the pies?	88
Sycamore	97
Hello Sailor	125
Skimmer Frame	129
Goldie	134
Fairy Tales	142

Contents

Idle Thoughts -- *poem*	iii
Introduction	17
Something they didn't have when you were young – *outburst*	21
Desire – *poem*	24
The Chicken Spit – *musing*	26
Menopausaurus – *outburst – poem*	29
Random – *musing – poem*	32
The Cool of the Evening – *musing*	34
Candy for Kids – *poem*	38
Approaching the Care Home – *poem*	40
In my Heaven there will be only Five Year Olds – *poem*	42
Raiders of the Lost Bark – *outburst – poem*	43
Christmas in a Traffic Jam – *musing – poem*	45
Season's Greetings – *playlet*	47
Nobody Really Cares – *poem*	50
A Snapdragon by any other Name – *musing*	51
London 2011 – *musing – poem*	58
London 2012 – *musing – poem*	59
Do Long Noses Run In Your Family? – *musing*	60
Your Nose... – *poem*	63
A Shaft of Wit – *musing*	64
The Curious Incident of the Toilet Brush in the Night Time – *musing*	68
Born Guilty *confessional – musing*	72
What Little Girls Are Made Of – *playlet*	78
Pooh Sticks – *musing*	82

Heimlich Manoeuvres in the Dark – *musing*	84
My Wife is a Small Woman – *musing*	89
Farewell Tour *reflective* – *musing*	92
Lost in Translation – *musing*	98
Offerings to 'The Meaning of Liff'	101
Flash Fiction	103
Strange Sayings	104
Birds and Bee – *story*	105
East of Ipswich – *musing*	111
One Shade of Grey – *story*	115
Bucket List *article*	118
Wacky Races – *poem*	127
Face Book – *poem*	130
Going Downhill Fast – *poem*	132
Fairy Tales and Scapegoats – *musing*	135
Here Endeth... – *musing*	138
The Language of God – *poem*	140
Faith and Fairy Tales – *musing*	143
Fateful – *musing*	145
The Scientists Roll of Faith – *outburst* – *poem*	146
Resolution – *story*	147
Shoddy Goods – *story*	150
Forget Me Not – *poem*	155
Impulse – *story*	157
Desperate Times – *story*	160
Chocolate *desperate* – *musing*	162
On the Seventh Day – *playlet*	166
Bread of Heaven – *playlet*	170
Floccinaucinihilipilification *article*	173
Argentine Tango a Mill and Boons romance by Tufty Woodcock – *story*	175
The Garden of Delights by Tufty Woodcock – *story*	178
Pisygod Wibblywobbly – *musing*	181

The Missing Link – *story*	186
Fall – *musing*	190
The White Lie – *poem*	192
The White Rose – *poem*	193
Keep Faith – *poem*	194

Peter Lancaster is a retired teacher who lives in the Greater Manchester area. He is the author of 'Up a Hill Backwards... and Other Pennine Ramblings', and the editor of 'A Small, Good Thing', by Poynton Creative Writers' Guild.

Introduction

This little collection of poems, stories, outbursts and musings is put forward as an homage to Jerome K. Jerome. His book, 'Idle Thoughts of an Idle Fellow', published in 1886, is like mine, a series of humorous articles on various subjects. Not that I claim to be anything like as good a writer as Jerome but at least I'm still 'above ground and moving', as they say.

What I admire and enjoy about Jerome's writing is his ability to make small, incidental things amusing. For instance, in 'Idle Thoughts of an Idle Fellow' he muses about whether it is wise to keep your hands in your trouser pockets. A mundane topic but Jerome manages to make it hilarious. He hints that there might be something inappropriate, even perverted, about putting your hands in your pockets. Jerome conveys the impression that he is an innocent at large, but a lot of intelligent design goes in to making his stories flow naturally. As he modestly observes in his preface,

'What readers ask nowadays in a book is that it should improve, instruct and elevate. This book wouldn't elevate a cow'.

He is underselling himself. He is quite able to make shrewd comments about the human condition such as,

'It is so pleasant to come across people more stupid than ourselves. We love them at once for being so.'

We chuckle at this and conclude that perhaps Jerome is being a bit harsh, but in a thought that definitely elevates he continues,

'It is in our faults and our failings, not in our virtues, that we touch one another and find sympathy. We differ widely enough in our nobler qualities. It is in our follies that we are as one.'

Jerome acknowledges his own shortcomings and extends a hand of good will to the reader, asking him to remember that we are all in the same boat.

I can identify with Jerome; his voice is there with me. I feel that he is standing looking over my shoulder as I write - no doubt with his hands in his pockets!

When I first researched Jerome's biographical details one website described his birth so:

'Jerome was born in Walsall, the fourth child of Jerome Clapp, who dabbled in architecture and Marguerite Jones'.

I am glad to see that any unfortunate misunderstanding has now been avoided by the addition of a comma after 'architecture'.

Jerome was not christened with his father's surname 'Clapp', for compelling reasons. Instead, his parents decided to repeat his first name as a surname, so that he became Jerome Jerome, and then as an afterthought, they put a 'K' in the middle. I suppose this was a gesture to the former 'Clapp', but they came up with some tale of it being after a certain Gyorgy Klapka, an exiled Hungarian general. I can't help thinking that his parents more than likely came to the realisation that Jerome Jerome sounds a bit stupid. At least his final appellation has the advantage of simply nominating the man as Jerome, without having to worry whether you are using his first or second names.

His father was a successful ironmonger and non-conformist preacher who, due to a series of bad investments, lost a great deal of money, forcing the thirteen year old Jerome to leave Grammar school in 1872, to help support the family through a series of menial jobs.

Nevertheless, Jerome managed to keep alive his literary ambitions and became a contributor of comic articles for the magazine 'Home Chimes'. This later was collated into the book: 'Idle Thoughts of an Idle Fellow', followed in 1889 by his most popular work, 'Three Men in a Boat', which made him well-known and financially secure.

In some ways my own life has mirrored Jerome's in that like him I have been an erstwhile thespian, teacher and writer. Also, we have both had itinerant jobs as packers or as persons who shovel things; and we have both enjoyed smoking pipes. Luckily, I didn't lose my parents in my teens or have to forego formal education to keep my family.

The lasting impression one receives of Jerome is that of a kindly, funny, clever, yet self-deprecating man. I am sure I cannot match these qualities, but like Jerome daffy things seem to keep happening to me and I feel compelled to write about them. My hope is that you will find parts of this book at least heading in Jerome's direction. As my first boss advised me shortly after I had started working for him,

'If you aim at the stars, Lancaster, you might just hit the lamp post'.

Something They Didn't Have When You Were Young

They say that the definition of technology is 'something they didn't have when you were young'. When our daughter was still a child we contemplated buying a garden slide for her – one of the self-assembly sort. Despite evidence to the contrary, I am actually quite handy at DIY, having made book shelves, wardrobes and hi-fi units in my time. However, the instruction manual for the assembly and maintenance of garden slides was something of a different order. It included a warning that 'to reduce the risk of serious injury or death' I must 'read and follow the instructions and refer to them often'. Hazards I might be inflicting upon an unsuspecting youngster included: 'serious head injury hazard', 'collision hazard', 'choking hazard' (which I imagined to be a child swallowing a loose screw whilst simultaneously sliding down wearing a plastic bag on their head); 'strangulation hazard' (presumably by a father who has reached his limit of endurance assembling the slide), and 'tip over hazard'. It was so complicated and time consuming. I worked out that I would be spending about one third of all my waking hours making sure a child could come to no harm on it – and I could never sleep at night again.

There were fourteen safe play instructions enjoining me to observe capacity limits – 'see front cover' (a picture of a solitary - rather nervous looking boy – braving the dangers of the slide); 'dress children well', teach children to 'sit in the centre of the slide', 'check for splintered wood' (what, every time?); verify that suspended climbing ropes, ladders, chains or cables were not about to create an 'entanglement hazard', and so on and so on – no open-toed sandals, flip flops or clogs (clogs?). I had become a gibbering wreck just reading the manual and decided to give our daughter a rabbit instead.

Things can take over your life you see. Surely, there must be a happy medium somewhere. Another example of mystifying modernity is the mobile phone. I have a very old cracked one which works but does not give me much 'street cred'. I have spent whole evenings sitting in the bosom of my family and never getting as much as a word from any of them as they all sit furiously texting and tweeting and goodness knows whatever else. I usually sit staring at the wall or talking to myself and remembering times when we used to have reasonably stimulating conversations together. 'No more', I said (to myself) one day. 'The next time my daughter gets an upgrade on her phone I am going to stake a claim for her old one'.

Thus it came to pass that one eventful evening I became the proud possessor of Katherine's cast off – a Desire S HTC smart phone. And smart I really felt with it attached to my ear. I could now be sophisticated, urbane; able to solve all the problems of the world. My daughter commented on how good I looked with it. In short, friends, I became proud, and we all know what pride comes before, don't we?

After only a couple of weeks with my new status symbol we were on holiday in Woodbridge, Suffolk in a small but trendy café. After coffee I needed to use the facilities and made tracks for the unisex lavatory on the premises. Being unisex the loo didn't have a urinal, only a WC and so, having obtained relief the usual way, I politely bent forward to lower the seat as the toilet flushed. All would have been well and I could have continued my life in a smart phone assured way if only I had not placed the wretched thing in my top pocket earlier. Faster and more slippery than an eel and with nary a sigh, it slipped soundlessly from my pocket as I stood contemplating the toilet and disappeared with enthusiasm down the U-bend, and so on into eternity. Plop went the phone, scream went I, down went my arm into the bowels of the drainage system, with no result except anxious enquiries from the café owner about my welfare. Alas, the only ring tone to be had if you call my Desire S, HTC these days is, 'Under the Sea' from 'The Little Mermaid'.

Desire

Elegant and slim you feel,
Smooth, black and easy to handle.
You tingle and agitate beneath my touch,
Illuminating bright new worlds
Of useful applications.
Desire S, HTC,
I dropped you down the toilet when going for a pee.

Satnav

The Chicken Spit

Although my parents didn't take The Daily Express, every Christmas they used to buy me the anthology of cartoons by Giles, the cartoonist for that publication. I remember being struck by one of Giles creations: namely, Grandma. Grandma was short and wide and wore a bombazine black overcoat at all times, set off by a fox fur round her neck and a battered, black bonnet. I suppose that the reason she made such an impact on me is that *my* grandmother looked identical to Giles's. Did I mention the walking stick, the half moon spectacles and the wrinkled stockings? Both grandmas had them.

Grandma used to come and stay with us from time to time. It gave opportunity for the kerfuffles to die down over some of her more extreme acts. For instance, if anyone had the temerity to park in front of her small back-to-back house in Brighouse she would march out and empty the dregs from her teapot all over the offending vehicle. I think she was nearly ninety by then but she was threatened with arrest by the police if she didn't desist.

When she visited, Grandma would talk incessantly; never really waiting for or wanting a response, partly because she was rather deaf. She would loom over me when I was happily playing with my toys and say things like,

'Man, love thyself!' Or, 'A bitter old woman is the Devil's crowning glory.'

She was cheerful like that.

When I say that Grandma had a walking stick I mean that it was a white stick, for as well as being partially deaf she was also partially sighted. To cross a road she would merely wave her stick at the traffic and launch herself across the street, bringing cars screeching to a halt.

However, she could see all right when she wanted to. In Macclesfield there used to be a shop called 'The Chicken Spit', which sold hardly anything other than roast chickens, cooked on the premises. Indeed, the main feature of the establishment was the very fine, multi-rung rotisserie machine, which was sited in the window, gently turning sizzling chickens a golden brown colour. The delicious smell wafted out onto the pavement and drew in many a passing customer, in those halcyon days before supermarkets.

One particular Saturday found me with my mum and dad and grandma, staring at the birds of' The Chicken Spit', and the two ladies became involved in important and complex discussions about which particular roasting fowl would be best for Sunday lunch. My father and I stood disconsolately next to them, shuffling our feet and looking a trifle bored, as we were excluded from this particular debate. The decision made, my mother entered the shop and joined the not inconsiderable queue waiting patiently to be served.

All would have been well if it were not that some diabolical individual in front of my mother suddenly pointed to the same chicken that we had decided was going to be ours. We couldn't hear the conversation going on inside but the shop assistant made as if to secure the chosen one. It was at this point that my grandma showed her true colours – the Yorkshire grit in her surfaced with a vengeance as she took her white walking stick and struck it forcibly on the plate glass window of 'The Chicken Spit', causing everyone to look up, startled, and the shop assistant to pause in shock. With all now suitably attentive, grandma glowered fiercely and mouthed at them

'That's *our* chicken!'

There was a hiatus whilst everybody collected their thoughts and then my father, who was normally such a capable sort of chap, simply turned and walked away, unable to cope with the embarrassment. My mother, who was a quiet and unassuming lady, looked as if she would like nothing better than for the floor to open up and swallow her. I, on the other hand, thought the whole thing hilarious and could only stagger off with tears of mirth in my eyes as my father returned to usher away the offending grandmother, who was still protesting loudly. My mother scuttled out of the queue and after us down the road.

The old 'Spit' isn't there anymore. I often wonder if its reputation started to go downhill after that day.

Idle Thoughts

I watched one of David Attenborough's documentaries recently about a newly discovered species of dinosaur called Titanosaurus. Well here is one I have discovered; I call it Menopausaurus!

Menopausaurus

There's a beast on the loose in our house,
Not a mouse,
Or a moose, nor a Tyrannosaurus,
But it bites just the same, for its teeth are a bane,
Oh beware, it's the Menopausaurus!

When we're watching TV, or we're taking our tea,
And oblivious to what may befall us,
Do not grimace or grin, at what just walked in,
Not my wife but the Menopausaurus.

Off it goes in a trance to some hormonal dance,
Roaring loud in a state of imbalance,
Do you think that it saw us and shortly will floor us?
Run and hide from the Menopausaurus.

There are tears, there is laughter,
Who knows *what* it is after,
Hard to say so I trawl my Thesaurus.
'Distraught' or 'embittered',
With 'nerves frayed or frittered',
'Not all human' is Menopausaurus.

Now I've just had a thought,
Would St John and his Wort,
Like St George strike the dragon before us?
Would he slash, would he slay the monster at bay?
'Please hurry', is what we all chorus.

Well the storm clouds are gone,
So can life carry on?
The return of the mum who adores us.
HRT is the thing and that's why we sing,
'It's goodbye to old Menopausaurus!'

Idle Thoughts

Dragonweld

Peter Lancaster

Sometimes it is hard to understand why things happen the way they do. Is there some plan or purpose behind it all? Perhaps we shall find out one day.

Random

I saw a pigeon killed today, run down.
A juggernaut with brow of Mars bore down,
And took it off from its perpetual round,
Of pecking cigarette butts on the ground.

My lunchtime stroll was interrupted so,
That in the pet shop I refrained to go.
I had intended to put down some seed,
Yet now from life it had been freed.
As 'swish' the reaper's sickle blade swung past,
Scooped it away to some divine repast.

In the twinkling of an eye its mate,
Stood apart bereft by fate,
Not a yard away it watched alone,
Alas too late, the bird had flown,
Beneath the axle of an instrument,
Whose only purpose was to move cement.

I wondered if the bird would miss,
The billing, cooing and the kiss,
All lovey-dovey in the nest,
Where they had raised their young or perched at rest.

Idle Thoughts

As witness to this hapless scene of waste,
I sought to leave the scene of crime in haste,
But lines from Blake confront the great I AM
Did He who made the tiger make the lamb?
Did He who made the hunted will the arrow?
Or Providence dictate the fall of sparrow?
Please let me see some purpose, Lord,
In all this random, harsh discord.

The Cool of the Evening

I believe that it has become fashionable these days for those in the know to change into pyjamas and dressing gown in the early evening, and then lounge around so attired until retiring to bed. I thought that I might give this a go, not wanting to appear out of touch or unfashionable. It had been a warm day followed by a lovely evening and so, after a suitably leisurely meal, I ventured out into the garden to view the fruits of my labour, walking barefoot on the grass, caressing the luminous rudbeckias and sniffing the perfume of the honeysuckle. 'Ah!' I mused, 'This must be how the father of mankind, Adam the gardener, felt taking the air in the cool of the evening and communing with his maker'.

Incidentally, I want you to be impressed by the fact that in late middle age I am still able to write this without resort to spectacles of any kind, although on a recent visit to the opticians I was assured that I really did need them. I proudly refused (having seen his prices) and left with said optometrist remarking sardonically to his receptionist,

'Mr Lancaster is going to struggle on'.

However, my short-sightedness, both literal and metaphorical, now rebounded upon me – in my very own garden. You must know that late summer is the time when our little arachnids are at their most active.

Idle Thoughts

Those most peculiar creations, spiders, are out in force, spinning webs to their hearts content. The Garden Orb Spider, as I have since learnt it is called, is particularly fond of making those high wires from bush to hedge, across the lawns and paths of many a British parterre. Sadly, our garden was no exception; silken webs and threads were plentiful.

If only I had followed the advice of the eye quack I would have been able to see these works of art spun by multiple legs. As it was, in the midst of deep contemplation I wandered into a very forest of them. They were on my face, in my ears and in my eyes. My mouth spluttered with cobwebs. I don't know who was more surprised to be in close proximity – the garden orb spider or me. There he sat looking at me on my dressing gown shoulder and there I stood regarding him with unfeigned terror. The neighbours must have got a shock if they happened to be watching the scene from the safety of their living rooms. Why did this normally sedate (not to say serene) person next door suddenly throw off his robe, shouting the while, and dance up and down on his gown? Was it some strange pagan ritual they might wonder, or had he gone stark, staring mad?

Trying to maintain a little dignity, I satisfied myself that there were no foreign bodies about my person and, robing again, I sauntered into the house as nonchalantly as I could. Thank goodness that was over. What could I have been thinking? I walked past Jane, who was on the phone, and into the hall where I could examine my attire in the mirror to check for any further evidence of alien bodies. All seemed well though and I casually put my hand in my dressing gown pocket – to affect a relaxed and sophisticated appearance again. Imagine my horror when I withdrew my hand to find a large spider's leg between my fingers? It was time to yell and disrobe once more, followed by a prolonged period of jumping up and down on my dressing gown, particularly the pockets. Jane looked slightly puzzled, but mostly understanding, as though this action was a commonplace occurrence in our household.

The final act of this short but vicious tragedy was for me to peer into the pocket of my now rather dirty garment only to find a somewhat squashy and pulpy stain that might once have been a Garden Orb Spider. So much for the cool of the evening!

Idle Thoughts

Web Mistress

Candy for Kids

When I was a child,
The sweet shop drew me in,
Its pink confection, sugar scented.
I was sorely tempted.
'Share', my mother said.

When I was young,
The girls they drew me in.
Their arms and dresses, perfume scented,
I was sorely tempted.
'Don't share', the preacher said.

When I was a man,
And proud of what I had,
My barns expanded, money scented.
I was sorely tempted.
'Share', the poor said.

When I was old,
I saw the world,
Jumping at my command,
My hand extended, power scented,
I was sorely tempted.
'Not fair!' the others said.

Idle Thoughts

Think Pink

Peter Lancaster

My mother suffered from Alzheimer's disease in the last stage of her life and it was painful to see her decline from a woman who took such pride in her appearance to someone sans teeth and sans every thing. There was just one bright moment and that was the time when I last saw her alive.

Approaching the Care Home

Meandering in a goldfish bowl,
A plate-glass window on the soul,
The old-timers,
The Alzheimers.
Drowning in a murky world,
No oxygen of thought impels,
Still by some goad they are compelled
To shuffle off the mortal round,
Shed memories like clothing on the ground.

Inside: the chintzy, shitty chairs,
Elegance in ammonia air.
And there is Mum,
A ragged doll,
Crushed in her usual Parker Knoll.

'Hello', I say but no response,
'Your hair needs doing, dear'.
Bedraggled now upon a shoulder,
That had once beguiled my father.

Time passes but before I go,
A ray of sunshine can be traced,
I'm recognised by troubled eyes.
'Bless you', she says and smiles and sighs,
Till under storm clouds she retreats,
Into a less familiar face.
'Bless *you*, Mum', I say. 'Bless *you*.
Here,
Or in a better place'.

Peter Lancaster

In My Heaven There Will Be Only Five-year Olds
(After Michel Quoist)

God says...
In my heaven there will be only five year olds,
Lumpy, wrinkled five year olds,
Entering with bent backs and feeble limbs.
Deaf and daft,
In wheelchairs or on crutches,
But with the eyes of a child,
So that when I look them in the face,
I will recognise them.

Idle Thoughts

I was irritated a few years ago when visiting Sutton Hoo in Suffolk, to find only plastic and cardboard replicas of the weapons and treasures of the great barrow. The real ones have all been taken to the British Museum in London. It prompted this diatribe – which contains a few reverential nods towards T.S. Eliot.

Raiders of the Lost Bark

(Sutton Hoo, Suffolk)

A cold coming we had of it,
Across the sea from Jutland.
The sails slapping and cracking in the wind,
And the oarsmen grunting, sweating,
Along the rolling waves.
The coastline rising up and falling down,
Would the Briton fight?
Or would he welcome us?
A crowd on shoreline congregated
Those from yonderland migrated.

Mostly we are farmers,
Looking for a place,
Unspoilt and danger free.
And there at last,
The tidal river estuary,
And trees which overhang the bank,
Still waters easy, warm and dank.

Peter Lancaster

The struggle though was hard,
Damp sod and stone to turn and plough,
Before the ground would yield its seed,
Our children's hungry mouths to feed.

After such a fight our king,
(His body failing fast)
Asked that they should rest him there,
In Saxon long boat, stout and yare.
Adorn him with some totems of his life:
Fond memories perhaps of sons and wife.

What strength of arms took this old ship,
From river and the village far below?
What treasures rich so deftly stored,
Arraigned about the sleeping lord?
What gold and silver ornament was brought?
To give him comfort in the star-cold night?
And what care taken then to give him sight,
Of the little kingdom he had wrought?

* * *

In broad daylight they came,
The raiders of the lost bark.
Down from London in imperial strength,
To plunder Sutton Hoo.
Untouched and unmolested,
In barrow bleak and dark,
Cradling the long-dead king,
The underworld-ly bark.
But in the twinkling of an eye,
The arrogance of empire pounced,
And spirited his essence far away,
Replacing it with plastic, paste and wood,
No doubt for the common good.

Christmas is an awful time for rushing about, particularly for shopping with its attendant traffic jams.

Christmas in a Traffic Jam

Stuck in a traffic jam,
I dream of Christmas, snowy white.
But heart's not here,
My racing mind on things to do,
Places to go,
Imagine parcels, Sellotape and bills,
The bells are ringing,
Just like tills.

Inside the snarled up cars,
The snarling people fret and fume,
Frantic mums,
So much to do,
In Ho-ho-ho,
Can it be you,
Shopping trolley world?

So lonely in the merriment,
I find a stranger's smile,
Kindly meant.

A card slips from its envelope,
Revealing wintry scenes,
Of cottages and Christmas trees,
From some time long ago.
A boy runs out into that snow,
A joyful licence to go wild,
I look inside me for that child.

Peter Lancaster

Rain runs down like Christmas tears,
Car windscreen reflects my fears.
As we inch to Bethlehem,
In a toxic, traffic jam.

Speaking of shopping at Christmas time...

Season's Greetings

(The two types of verse should be read by different people – the scriptures by one person and the other verse by a chorus. The choral verses should be chanted, something like the rhythm of a train)

It's Christmas!

(chorus)

Got to get to Tesco's, got to get to Marks,
Flying down the by-pass, lining up to park.
Swivelling the trolley, snarling at the queues,
Piling on the turkey, crackers and the booze.

(This chorus is repeated at the end of each scripture reading in addition to each new chorus)

And in that region there were shepherds out in the fields, keeping watch over their flocks by night. And an angel of the Lord appeared to them and said, 'Be not afraid for behold I bring you good news of great joy which will come to all the people. For to us is born this day a Saviour , who is Christ the Lord.'

(chorus)

Lots of frowning faces, lots of worried looks,
Get the latest Tablet, microwave and books.
Got to get a big tree 50 metres high,
With forty thousand flashing bulbs lighting up the sky.

And suddenly there was with the angel a multitude of the heavenly host praising God and the glory of the Lord shone around them. 'Glory to God in the highest, they said, and on earth peace among men with whom he is pleased.'

(chorus)

Make the office party, now I don't feel well,
Wife is very angry, did that perfume smell?
Mum is looking stressed out, Dad is feeling poor,
Now those wretched carol singers knocking at the door.

Behold, an angel of the Lord appeared to Joseph in a dream saying, 'Son of David do not fear to take Mary as your wife for that which is conceived in her is of the Holy Spirit. She will bear a son, and you will call his name Jesus, for he will save His people from their sins.'

(chorus)

Santa Claus must help me, and his little elves.
Are there any I-pads still left on the shelves?
Then the Christmas argument, we sulk and scream and shout,
But isn't that what Christmas time is really all about?

Idle Thoughts

For to us a child is born to us a Son is given. His name will be called Wonderful Counsellor,
Mighty God, Everlasting Father, Prince of Peace.
Prince of Peace,
Of Peace
Of Peace
Peace.

Peter Lancaster

Nobody Really Cares

Nobody really cares you know.
Nobody really knows you care.
You care for nobodies really,
Really care.
You who knew care,
You really care,
For me.

Idle Thoughts

A Snapdragon by any other Name

Grosvenor Place, London. It sounded like an impressive location to me. Linked with the Dukes of Westminster, the Earls Grosvenor and the Viscounts Belgrave, its pedigree was impeccable. Couple that with a smart W1 postcode and some elegant Regency buildings that house embassies and swish hotels - you couldn't really go wrong, could you?

The pictures of the hotel fitted perfectly with the images already in my head of how Grosvenor Place should look. They showed a grand entrance with wide stone steps and a portico leading up to a large front door with a polished brass knob and letter box. Inside the lobby boasted marble floors, sweeping stairs and an imposing mirror, in front of which was displayed a huge bouquet of, what looked like, snapdragons.

I could imagine the bowing flunkeys deferentially carrying my suitcase whilst making polite enquiries after my well-being; the soft titters that greeted my charming and witty replies and the sweet scent of snapdragons filling my nostrils. Why was it so cheap? A 'Billy Bargain' as a friend of mine would say. I booked straightaway.

Arriving in London for a short break after a period of many years, Jane and I felt like a couple of hayseeds just blown in from the provinces. But once we had got the hang of the oyster cards for travelling the tube we soon began to act like old hands of the metropolis, rushing importantly onto the platforms wearing an impassive expression, save for a small, sardonic smile playing about the mouth and a raised nose or eyebrows when engaging in necessary exchanges.

The tube soon took us to Marble Arch, close to Grosvenor Place, and we wheeled our cases along the street looking for our hotel. The signs were good. We passed the Irish Embassy and then the Churchill Hotel, where an Arab sheikh was disembarking from a luxury charabanc with his entourage and several lorry-loads of luggage.

Soon enough we reached our destination and, at first glance, everything appeared to be just as it did on the brochure. There was the grand entrance, leading into the tastefully decorated lobby, and there was the mirror with the snapdragons and the chrysanthemums. I looked around for a bowing flunkey but could find only a sign pointing out that reception was downstairs – in the basement as it transpired. Still, never mind. We descended some narrow steps to the basement and were greeted (somewhat diffidently, I thought) by a receptionist, who immediately demanded full payment in advance of our stay. Not to be put off I paid up cheerfully and then waited expectantly for some service.

'Here your key. You Room 32,' said the man conducting our transaction, and he threw a plastic card on the desk, along with my debit card.

Now I had asked for a quiet room but, apparently, this couldn't be attained until you reached the fifth floor of the establishment -out of earshot I suppose- ten flights of stairs up from where we stood. If I said we were a trifle out of breath by the time we reached the fifth floor that would be an understatement; we were wheezing, sweating wrecks. The stairs became more precipitous the higher we climbed, twisting this way and that. To be fair the man at reception had helped us with our cases or, honestly, I don't think we would have made it.

'Here is room,' he announced. 'This is cupboard.' He threw open built-in doors on the small landing. I viewed our considerable height and said the first thing that came into my head.

'Where's the fire escape?'

'Excuse me?' he asked, looking puzzled.

'The fire escape,' I repeated, 'In case of an emergency, you know? How do we get out?'

The man pointed vaguely in the direction of some iron rungs attached to the wall which disappeared into the roof space.

'This is ladder,' he said, and then, apparently satisfied with his explanation he swiped the door to the room with the plastic card and proudly indicated for us to enter.

'You like.' It came out as a statement rather than a question.

We entered the room, which was very large but very basic. There was something of the garret about it.

The ghosts of serving maids from times past fluttered around the lace-curtained sash windows and I was tempted to look under the bed for stowaways. There was a kitchen sink and counter with a fridge under it, and what seemed to be an ancient portable air-conditioning unit squatted unhelpfully in the centre of the floor. The beds were all right except that one of them abutted the sash window and the window had been opened from the bottom, so that if you rolled over the wrong way in your sleep you would plummet peacefully to an untimely end five storeys down.

The piece de resistance had to be a block of electric extension sockets which had been glued to the kitchen counter, between the sink and the kettle. If you didn't suffer death by falling out of bed or by tripping over the air-conditioning unit then you were most likely to electrocute yourself spilling water onto the extension sockets. In short the whole place was a death trap. Jane was glowering quite hard by now.

'Why did you book this place?' she asked, and then answered herself, 'Because, as usual, it was cheap.'

I protested my innocence and agreed to calm her fears by checking out our escape route, in case of the fairly likely incidence of emergency. I retreated out onto the landing and regarded the iron rung ladder suspiciously. It was vertical, high and narrow and finished at a hatch in the ceiling. Well, if we were going to have trouble then this way out had to be explored, I reasoned and, taking hold carefully, I levered myself upwards. At the ceiling the ladder stopped at what appeared to be a dead end, until you craned your neck

180 degrees when a low, dark passageway became visible with a small bolted door at the end.

Twisting myself like a monkey I managed to make the transition from ladder to passage, though it was only passable on hands and knees. Feeling a bit claustrophobic I scrambled along till I made the door and with some difficulty unbolted it. It swung open onto the roof and light flooded the blackness, disorientating me. After a moment or two my eyes adjusted and I could make out a narrow ledge to my right, with a similar small door to the one I had just opened at the far side. To the front was a dizzying drop of perhaps one-hundred feet to the taxis and double-decker buses of Grosvenor Place. What an excellent fire exit I thought!

Retreating with some difficulty I retraced my path backwards to the hatch and then squeezed through and down the ladder to the landing. How on earth was I going to sell this one to Jane? Then I hit upon an idea. Before I went back to the bedroom I quickly ran down the stairs to the entrance lobby and, making sure there was no one looking, I deftly took a couple of the snapdragons out of their display and laboured back upstairs again. I entered the bedroom in triumph bearing my impromptu bouquet proudly, and proffered it to my long suffering spouse.

'The fire exit is not so bad,' I lied. 'And look what I found, just for you.'

Jane regarded the snapdragon. She had always liked flowers and I hoped this one might mollify her. Her tone softened somewhat but she still had things to say.

'Do you call this room, this hotel and those wretched flowers Grosvenor Place luxury?'

I thought quickly.

'Oh,' I remarked, as casually as I could, 'what's in a name? A snapdragon by any other name would smell as sweet.'

Jane took the snapdragons cautiously and sniffed them before flinging them to one side.

'Not when they are plastic,' she said.

Idle Thoughts

Snapdragon

Peter Lancaster

London 2011

Johnson said that the man who is tired of London is tired of life.
But I think it is London that is tired of life.
Greeting each new day with a grimy and unsmiling face,
Eyes fixed ahead in search of some new thing,
To divert it from the weight of years and stale air,
Exhaled from the lungs of the underground.
Ground down.

London Olympics 2012

Scrubbed up,
Dressed up,
As fresh, pretty and inviting as a bride,
London gleams on the world.
Guides stand as comfortably as Big Ben,
Smiling, talking, quite un-London like.
Proud of all that has been spent,
Achievement.

Peter Lancaster

Do Long Noses Run in your Family?

I wouldn't really call Tina Cushing my first girlfriend because she lived just across the way from me and we were thrown together from the age of three – playing cowboys and Indians or dabbling and dredging in the local stream. After her there was Tess. I was eleven by now and Tess let me push her on the swing in the local park. The girl I really liked was Susan Gregory but she seemed unattainable to me. I just didn't know how to tell her that I had a crush on her. No, my first girlfriend has to be Caroline (I forget her second name). She was the one I asked out. Technically it was she who asked me out, via a relay of messages conveyed by various third parties.

We were in the Parish Youth Club, that hotbed of passion and vice of 1960s Cheadle Hulme. Despite being fourteen I was still terrified of going and had to be ushered in by several mates. The building was an old Nissan hut, probably full of asbestos and other noxious substances, but it contained girls as well, who only appeared to be noxious in the sense that I was frightened to go near them. John and Titch had invited me several times and eventually I plucked up the courage to say yes. For the occasion I had my mother buy me a white polo neck jumper which I thought just the thing and it boosted my confidence somewhat, only

Idle Thoughts

for it to be dashed on receiving the information from John that only homosexuals wore white.

I was, therefore, sweating rather as I stepped over the portals of the church-blessed discotheque that was 'The Parish', to be met by loud music blaring from some ancient stereogram. It was presided over by a youth worker, who occasionally bellowed indecipherable and distorted sounds into an equally ancient microphone. The lights were dim and the floor was awash with teenagers; some dancing, some drinking soft drinks, but mostly just eyeing up one another and whispering conspiratorially to their friends.

I don't how long I stood trying to look cool and not homosexual, but after some time a girl of about my age rushed over importantly and muttered something to John. John raised his eyebrows slightly as he listened but apart from that he remained stony faced, as if he were receiving grave news about the medical condition of a relation of mine. The girl finished her message and scampered away. John approached me and bent close to my ear to inform me in sombre tones the impossibly exciting yet petrifying news that Caroline wanted to go out with me... and what was to be my answer? This was it, I must show no weakness. I nodded as nonchalantly as I could and stared in the general direction of Caroline's pack.

My acceptance was duly conveyed and, after what seemed like an age, another messenger approached to say that Caroline wanted walking home. 'Oh, walking home is it?' I said to myself, perspiring so heavily that I practically planed out of the door after the girl. Once in the open I was able get a proper impression of my date. From memory she was quite tall, yet slight, and wearing an off the shoulder white dress. She had short, bobbed blond hair and pink lipstick, but the overall effect for me was spoiled in large measure by a long thin nose that dominated her face. Don't get me wrong, I was certainly not on the back row when they handed out the large noses but this one was quite a statement. I stared haplessly until I felt it incumbent upon me to say something or do something but I didn't know what. Finally, I blurted out, 'Do long noses run in your family?' which probably wasn't the best chat up line so I grabbed her hand and we headed off up the road at a tremendous pace.

Caroline motioned the direction she lived then we walked silently, hand in hand, staring ahead like rabbits caught in headlights. After about a mile and a half she stopped outside a small corner house on the main road. She turned and looked at me and said, 'My hand won't fall off if you let go of it', and with that she disengaged and stamped off up the drive, nose first, before slamming the front door after her. I was still gawping, uncertain what to think or do, when the door flung open and there stood a man in his shirt sleeves, holding a newspaper and staring suspiciously in my direction. This I took to be Caroline's father although what really clinched it was the nose. It was long and upturned and, in the glare of the security lights, I could just make out a great dew drop, like a glacier mint, hanging perilously on its tip. I turned away from the hard stare of the man and set off for home, reflecting upon the fact that in more senses than one, long noses really did run in the family.

Your Nose...

Your nose is not pretty,
But retrouche and fun.
It turns up completely,
Yet still it's not done.
It looks like a strawberry,
All spotty and red,
And some folk might say,
That they'd rather be dead.
But your nose is to me,
So attractive and elegant,

Because as you see,
I'm an African elephant.

A Shaft of Wit

Autumn, I think, is my favourite season – when the full splendour of nature expresses itself in the fruits and seeds of the forest and the field; when the bough groans on the apple tree and the blackberries burst forth amidst the brambles, satisfying the blackbird, the tit, and even the passing Reynard. What simple pleasure is to be taken observing the squirrels hiding their nuts in grass. And oh, how one longs to run around the garden as nature intended, smeared in blackcurrant juice, for the sheer joy of celebrating the bounty of Mother Earth; to observe the myriad leaves fall from the trees to the ground … and then to observe them clogging up the drains on the house. What? Wretched season! You can keep your mists and mellow fruitfulness; the driveway and guttering overflow with rotting vegetation.

My usual way of dealing with this detritus of the aptly named 'Fall' is to rush frantically round the lawn sporting a besom (I said 'besom' not 'bosom'), brushing the leaves into small mountains, and then raging impotently as the wind catches them and sends them scurrying back to their original places. This year it has been particularly problematic - the leaves rustling with stifled laughter as they whirlwind around me, refusing point blank to be collected and blowing vigorously in my face at the very point of being tipped from shovel to Wheelie Bin.

Idle Thoughts

But I have to tell you, I am a resourceful human being with all the cunning of a Reynard myself. There must be a better way I thought, as I picked out bits of moss and worm from my mouth and leant on my besom. Then I noticed the lawnmower, slumbering gently in its winter bed in the greenhouse, put away for the year, its labours completed. Or so it imagined. Bingo! A shaft of wit caught my imagination. If the lawnmower could suck up grass cuttings then could it not also pick up leaves? Quickly, I unravelled the wire, plugged in and wheeled the mower onto the lawn, surprising two mice which were happily hibernating in the box.

The neighbours probably thought it a little odd to hear the sound of an electric lawnmower in November but I suppose that, after several years of being in close proximity to me, they are used to certain eccentricities on my part.

At first, the system worked perfectly - leaves flew into the box of the mower in great multitudes and, even better, they were so compacted by this operation that they proved easy to deposit in the bin. Soon, great swathes of green appeared in the carpet of gold and brown. At this rate the leaf problem would be over before lunch. And why stop with the grass? We have large trees that overhang the pavement and create messy deposits for pedestrians. Could not the rotary lawnmower glide over a hard surface just as easily? You see how I get carried away with enthusiasms.

The whole scheme went like clockwork. With the extension lead in place I ran up and down the pavement clearing leaves, chewing gum, and dog dirt (poo!). All went into the box, and subsequently the bin.

My excitement at success knew no bounds. When the pathways were clear I steered the mower into the gutter and proceeded up and down the road. In no time the grass, the pavements and even the gutters were sparkling clean and free of mess. But then, dear reader, without bothering to stop and consider I aimed the mower at the floor of our garage where sundry leaves lurked, brought in on our feet or by the wind. Two more seconds and I would be done - leafless!

In my opinion, the manufacturers of lawnmowers missed a trick when they clearly failed to envisage that people might want to mow their carpets. You see, there were bits of old carpet in the garage and, I speak frankly to you, the mower did not react kindly to being asked to trim them. Actually, there was a sickening crunch, followed by a high-pitched whine, and then silence, the machine expired, choked to death on Axminster.

That is one of the ironies of life. Just as I thought that the excesses of nature had been conquered and subdued, to be hoist by my own petard - or carpet in this instance; not so much a shaft of wit but a waft of s***.

Idle Thoughts

Leucanthemum vulgare
(Moon Daisy)

Peter Lancaster

Like all the musings in this book, I am afraid this is a true story.

The Curious Incident of the Toilet Brush in the Night Time

Baby monitors have been around in one form or another since the 1930s, but they didn't really enter *my* consciousness until we had a baby of our own. After carefully switching on the transmitting device in the room of our sleeping infant for the first time, my wife and I tiptoed across the landing into our own bedroom, where the receiver was sited. The sound of baby's murmurs and various bodily functions were transmitted and transmuted to us as strange, amplified electronic noises, in much the same way that I imagine a hearing-aid to function.

At first we were glued to the receiver, nervously interpreting each sound as some sort of warning of trouble, but after several checks on the baby we settled down to our own rest. Some time later we were both awakened simultaneously by the sound of adult voices coming through the monitor. Groggily trying to tune in to the conscious world, we couldn't help but listen to what seemed to be some sort of whispered conversation between two men.

'You go for the jewellery Sid, and I'll get the silverware.'

'Righto, Dick. You take the sack.'

Jewellery and silverware? I didn't know that we had any but we were left in no doubt that some sort of burglary was underway on the premises. And then there was the baby...! I leapt out of bed, stark naked and scurried round the bedroom looking for a weapon to combat the intruders. Finding nothing I ran into the en suite and tried there. A safety razor perhaps or a rubber duck? There was nothing, absolutely nothing lethal, apart from potions that might poison you. But how would I persuade burglars to drink them? Desperate, I seized the only thing that looked able to be wielded – a toilet brush – and armed with that I strode boldly onto the landing, pausing only momentarily when I caught a ghostly reflection of myself in the wardrobe mirror. Staring back at me was a pale figure (possibly male) wearing only a moustache, with matching toilet brush bristles. If I presented a sight that would stop burglars in their tracks, it would be largely for reasons of novelty rather than from the fact that I posed some sort of threat to them. Nevertheless, the baby was in danger, and so I threw open the door of her room and charged in, emitting a noise somewhere between a hoarse shriek and a squeal, ready to defend my goods and chattels.

The baby woke and started to cry as I flicked on the light and prepared to engage in a duel to the death, but there were no signs of any robbers or kidnappers - nothing indeed out of place or disturbed. Where were they? I hunted about fruitlessly for some sign until I heard voices again, coming from the baby monitor.

'You can hear the next episode of, 'Robbery at the Grange', at the same time on Monday night, here on Radio Four.'

Above the sounds of my daughter screaming (either at the noise of her father or at the sight of him) my brain gradually worked out the truth of the matter – that the baby monitor had somehow picked up a national radio station. As Jane cooed and cuddled our baby girl back to sleep I couldn't help wondering if this experience might scar her for life... or me.

Idle Thoughts

Hi!

Born Guilty

When I was quite young some friends and acquaintances persuaded me it would be a good idea for me to join them in playing on a local building site. The site, which was soon to become a housing estate, offered uncommon pleasures for boys. Soon we were walking up gangways and swinging from unfinished stairwells; lobbing bricks from upstairs windows and, generally, having a 'smashing' time.

Of course, it is very easy to get absorbed in such shenanigans, to the extent that when the heavy hand of a night watchman landed on my shoulder I was as surprised and hooked as a fish enjoying bait at the end of a fishing line. I can't remember exactly what he said but he was obviously very angry and he soon had us all rounded up and in a row, listening to him rant about how evil we were. I have always hated being told off. It is not just the idea of being caught out and punished for doing wrong that I hate, but also the shame of being exposed as a wrong doer in front of the world.

This all goes back to the time when I was three or four years old and in hospital to have a key removed from my windpipe. I had been running around the house with my friend Simon, pretending to be a Red Indian but somehow I had got hold of an alarm clock and was holding it above my face as we whooped and made war cries. Why a Red Indian would be brandishing an alarm clock I don't know but it seemed

Idle Thoughts

to fit in. Unfortunately, the key was still in the back of the clock and, when I was in the middle of emitting a particularly blood-curdling scream, it fell off the winder and disappeared down my throat. In an instant I went from Hiawatha screaming to Hiawatha choking, and the world seemed to go into slow motion. My mother was in the kitchen nearby, nervously listening to Simon's mother cluck away about Mrs So-and-so and Mr What's-his-name, but the sound of her son gurgling and spluttering grabbed her attention.

The poor woman really didn't know what to do and went into some sort of paralysis. I can vaguely recall her wide-eyed and panicked expression as she stared at me, open-mouthed. Thankfully, Simon's mother was not so disabled and she leapt towards me, with remarkable speed for a woman of her hen-like proportions, and proceeded to thump me vigorously on the back. She must have loosened something because a moment or two later I swallowed hard and immediately stopped choking, and started hiccoughing instead. I hiccoughed repeatedly at frequent intervals but at least I wasn't dead – that seemed to be the main thought at the time.

I didn't stop hiccoughing, however. I was hiccoughing when my father got home from work and he peered down my throat, with little efficacy. My parents tried all the old remedies for hiccoughs – they tried to surprise me; they told me to hold my breath; they got me to drink water holding my nose but all to no avail. After a few days of hiccoughing and, I suspect, sifting carefully through my motions for any sign of a key, it was off to see the 'Quack', as my father called the doctor. Our doctor was a very dour Scottish gentleman who always wore a dark brown three-piece suit. He lived in a dark brown house and worked in a dark brown study that smelled of tobacco, which meant that his fingers were a sort of yellowy brown as well. This was particularly unpleasant if he happened to have them halfway down your oesophagus looking for lost keys.

'I see it,' he announced in a tombstone voice. 'I am afraid he will have to go to hospital.'

This was a pronouncement both grave and of immense consequence. Hospital! I didn't know what hospital was but it sufficiently concerned my mother for me to pick up her unhappiness.

It was with some sense of unease that I found myself the following day in the children's ward of Stockport Infirmary. Parents were not allowed to stay with their offspring and I was left to it – inside a large cot with only my toy cars to keep me company. When I stood up and held onto the bars of my cot I could see other children, similarly caged, dotted around this enormous room, too far away for me to make contact. Anyway, they didn't seem very lively to me and so I entertained myself by running my cars up and down the blankets on the bed. I had no idea what they were going to do to me to remove the key and no one came to explain the matter – or to explain anything else if it comes to that. They certainly didn't explain the toilet arrangements and, age three, I lacked the social graces to politely ask if I might be excused. It wasn't a problem; I just went in the bed. Suddenly, I had a lumpy obstacle course over which to push my Dinky toys which pleased me, with only the occasional bad smell escaping to give me pause for thought.

It must have given the nursing staff pause for thought because, after a while, one of them came sniffing over and lifted the sheets of the bed cautiously back. If I had lacked attention before I certainly got it now. The linen was ripped away amidst cries of disgust and I was hauled into the air, stark naked, and paraded up and down in front of my sick companions.

'Look at this dirty little boy,' said the nurse, swinging me back and forth at arms length.

'Just look at what he's done!'

With some instinctive insight into the guilt and consequent shame of my situation I was hauled over to the sluice in the nurses' room and washed down, unceremoniously. I had not said a word. I knew somehow that I was a deeply bad boy and the subsequent appearance of a lollipop in my hand only contrived to confuse me.

I suppose the fact that I can remember this incident so clearly more than half a century later serves to prove the impact it must have made on me and how it formed the basis for many future reactions to events in my life – like the fear and humiliation of being caught by the caretaker of the building site. That scenario soon became much worse when the man spotted a policeman cycling past. He hailed him over and I died inside as the 'Bobby' dismounted from his bike and walked towards us with that weighty gravitas police are able to invest in their gait. Reaching our line of trapped boys he solemnly pulled out a notebook and pencil and began to take down our details. This was too much for me; the tears flooded down my face and I would have confessed to anything at that point. After the appalling evil of our crime had been recorded forever in his book of judgement the blackly clad and helmeted officer of the law proceeded to give us all a good wigging before eventually releasing us to crawl home separately, unable to talk to our parents so heavy was our guilt.

Idle Thoughts

Petal

This sketch was inspired by a psychological experiment conducted on television to compare the thought processes of little boys with those of little girls. They gave the little boy a bag of sweets and left them both in a room. What follows is essentially the result!

What Little Girls Are Made Of

(We discover a little boy (LB) sitting at a table with some sweets on it. He is counting the sweets. A little girl (LG) enters and sits on a chair next to the little boy. She watches him a moment and then speaks)

LG: Hello.

LB: (after a moment} Hello.

LG: What's your name?

LB: Fred.

LG: My name is Jenny. (pause) What you got there then?

LB: Sweets.

LG: Hmmm! They look nice. (pause) Why aren't you eating them?

LB: My mum gave them to me … they've got to last.

LG: How long?

LB: Dunno.

LG: Well suppose she's got some at home.

LB: She has!

LG: Hmm, well suppose you eat these, what will your mum do?

LB: Dunno.

LG: Will she give you some more sweets?

LB: (thinking hard) She might.

LG: She will.

LB: I suppose so.

LG: (after a pause) Can I have one - because your mum will give you more?

LB: (struggling with the complexity of the issue) All right, just one.

(The little girl takes a sweet and eats it with relish. LB counts his sweets again. Pause)

LG: Hmmm. Am I your friend, Fred?

LB: Dunno.

LG: I am aren't I? I am your friend, Fred.

LB: I suppose so.

LG: (pause) If I'm your friend you should share things with me.

LB: I suppose.

LG: We should share all sorts of things ... like sweets.

LB: Sweets?

LG: Will you share your sweets with me, Fred?

LB: No!

LG: Go on … just one. You said I was your friend. Go on, one more!

LB: All right – one more. (The little girl takes a sweet and eats it with relish. Pause)

LG: Fred?

LB: What?

LG: I love you.

LB: (incredulous) What?

LG: (giggles) Do you want to be my boy friend?

LB: Dunno. What do I have to do?

LG: Share! (she snatches the whole bag of sweets)

Idle Thoughts

Power Play

Peter Lancaster

Pooh Sticks

It is that time of year when the geese migrate to other climes. Squawking[1] and honking they pass in great skeins over our house, bombing indiscriminately all over my clean car. Their honking seems to mock me as I shake my fist impotently at them.

Impotent, now that's a word you don't want to hear; that your potency has migrated south, like everything else about you. Take my hair for instance. Well, somebody has taken it as you see. I sometimes wonder if the geese are preparing my bald pate as a future target. But the hair has not gone entirely – some of it has migrated too, down my body. Don't ask, except that when I go to a barber these days he asks if I would like my back styling.

It is all part of the process I'm afraid; the way things are ordained; sans eyes, sans teeth, sans everything. But don't worry; the government has devised a way to liven up your life. When you hit sixty they send you a little kit in the post which turns out to be tools and equipment necessary to obtain a sample; yes that's right – a stool sample; a crap, a turd, a load of ... well you know what. Apparently, to take a sample of the aforementioned substance all you need is a stick, an

---

[1] It has been pointed out to me that geese don't squawk. I put the word in for reasons of literary effect. Perhaps they had kidnapped a chicken.

envelope and ... that's about it; plus some instructions on the consistency of poo they require; small, medium or large, beginning, middle and end.

It's all very technical except that they don't really tell you how to obtain the sample. Oh yes, they say how they will examine it in a laboratory to discover if you have some wasting disease, very responsible of course, but they don't tell you how to collect or bag it (nor do I really fancy licking the envelope). So I sit miserably thinking about it but not doing it, as it were.

A story has it that people in Bury are ineligible for the test because they eat so much Black Pudding that their stools already contain blood and consequently the readings would be false (an urban myth I suspect). Before the advent of main drains, excrement was collected into wagons by blokes with great long ladles, who scooped it up to be spread on the fields as fertiliser; a bit smelly I imagine but a regular job. They were called the night-soil men. My father-in-law worked in a factory where the toilet cleaner was looked down upon and mocked by the other workers. 'You can laugh,' retorted the cleaner. 'It may be just shit to you, but it's my bread and butter'.

As for the geese, the swallows and particularly the people who migrate, floating like Pooh Sticks helplessly across water, we must do what we can. If we are not able to help everyone at least let us not be found on the side of the mockers. Remember, at some stage we all migrate to another plane, leaving behind merely fertiliser.

Peter Lancaster

Heimlich Manoeuvres in the Dark

If you are anything like me then you must often have watched television programmes about first-aid which show you how to deal with 101 things that might go wrong in everyday situations; how to fix a splint, make a sling, for example, or perform mouth to mouth resuscitation perhaps. And then there is that bizarre procedure called the Heimlich Manoeuvre, designed to alleviate the sufferings of someone choking on a bone, a boiled sweet or suchlike. Probably your response at seeing someone being brought back to life by a quick jab in the stomach left you determined to set about organising a suitable course for yourself at night school or the St John's Ambulance, in order to acquaint yourself with Herr Heimlich's famous manoeuvre.

My response, however, was to feel vaguely guilty in the knowledge that I wasn't going to do anything about it. At the end of the day I was going to chance it – to rely on the fact that no one I knew was about to swallow a chicken bone, or if they did then there would be competent medical practitioners close at hand to deal with the problem, without me having to go to the trouble of actually doing something myself. There you have it, if I am to be brutally honest.

This theory worked fine for years. I didn't feel any inadequacy when out for a meal or eating at home.

Idle Thoughts

Maybe I would pause occasionally before stuffing my face with a pork sandwich or a sausage roll, perchance glancing around to see whether help was available if required, but beyond that no desire troubled me to swat up on medical procedures first touched upon during my time with the scouting organisation. That is until my wife, recently returned from a business trip and (rather hurriedly) consuming a pie that I had baked specially for her, started to cough and choke, in a frankly alarming not to say inconvenient way because I could no longer hear the television properly.

Jane: 'I'm choking!'

Me: 'Are you choking?'

Jane: '(cough, choke) Help!'

Me: 'Do you want help?'

Jane: (gets up and runs around the room)

Me: 'Are you okay?'

Jane: 'I can't breathe.'

Me: 'Can't you breathe?'

Jane: 'Gurgle.'

Me: 'Do you want me to do anything?'

No answer. Jane was bent double trying to bring up the offending foreign body. She pointed to her back and then her stomach and then ululated in a circle, as if demonstrating an Indian war dance.

Jane: (whispering terminally) 'Heimlich!'

Me: 'Do you want me to perform the Heimlich Manoeuvre?'

Jane: 'Gasp!'

Although still not entirely sure I took Jane's reactions to be affirmative enough and so, reluctantly turning off 'Cash in the Attic', I positioned myself behind her stooping figure and gingerly put my hands round her in the general region of her stomach. My mind flitted back to the first aid classes at 2nd Handforth Scout Group's hut, circa 1965, but nothing helpful popped up. It meandered mistily onto Ray Mears clearly demonstrating the Heimlich Manoeuvre in the backwoods of North America, but all he was saying to me was 'Blah, blah, blah!' A creaking sort of dying sound emanating from Jane finally concentrated my mind and I suddenly launched into action and began pulling my clenched fists into her abdominal areas whilst at the same time pumping vigorously at her rear. I don't really know what effect this had on my better half because I couldn't see her face but panic had finally descended upon me.

I think it was the neighbour's astonished face staring at us through the front window that made me reconsider momentarily, and at the same moment the ill-defined, soupy thoughts that had been floating round my brain came to rest on the words 'bay leaf'. You see I had doubted all along that there had been a bone in the reconstituted, mushy meat from the supermarket that had gone into the pie, but there had been a bay leaf or two. Of course it was one of the sharp, prickly spines of the dry laurel that was causing the problem. Just then Jane gave an almighty cough and ejected an unidentified object from her mouth, catapulting it across the living room. I scampered over to the offending article and picked it up.

'As I thought, darling' I pronounced lightly, 'You see you weren't really in danger of choking, it was just a bay leaf.'

Jane considered me a moment from the floor, where she had gently wilted, before delivering her verdict on the whole episode. You know I don't really understand women sometimes. You'd think I had done something wrong. It all goes to show that you should pay great attention to TV.

Who nicked all the pies?

My Wife is a Small Woman

One of life's more exacting experiences for me is having to deal with things that break, rot, languish or generally collapse in the home. How many of us have stood anxiously by whilst a plumber stares down a blocked toilet and announces in a grave tone,

'Hmmm, I'm afraid this is not going to be cheap.'

Or maybe we have suddenly been thrown into complete darkness by a fuse going bang somewhere, leaving us poised on the stairs, not daring to move, or sorting through some paperwork, reading a book and/or sitting on the loo. We are helpless and left merely to curse ineffectually at the unfairness of the universe in general and our power supplier in particular.

Things are usually compounded by my fanciful notion that I am somewhat of a handyman. This is especially true when I consider how much money I might save by doing a job myself.

Airily brushing aside my wife's protestations, I declare that the tradesman's estimate is ridiculous and puffing out my chest I start to assemble my ragbag of tools for the required repair. It is a disaster waiting to happen, like playing with matches in a fireworks factory. As I put on my work clothes I start to feel like a proper man at last – not effetely tapping away at a keyboard but wrangling and wrestling in a macho way with the metaphorical steer that is a faulty gasket or leaning bookshelf. I adopt a steely expression, chew gum and start to swear a bit (although I draw the line at spitting) because these are the manly, workmanlike things one does.

Ripping things apart is always the easy bit. When we needed a new kitchen, I was itching to get started on crowbarring the old one out. All went well and soon the garden was full of worktops, base units and the proverbial kitchen sink, ready to be broken up and skipped. But as I swung my lump hammer at one of the plastic legs of a carcass it suddenly shattered into a thousand pieces and a shard arced through the air like shrapnel before hitting my eyeball. Fortunately, the shard bounced out again but my eye filled with blood and Jane was confronted with something like Frankenstein's monster growling and howling and bleeding all over the furniture.

A quick trip to A and E confirmed that there was no lasting damage but after that I wasn't allowed to go anywhere near the kitchen. A professional fitter was employed and I had to content myself by sulking whilst making him cups of tea. The day came when the work surfaces were to be installed. Jane had already left for work and I had an important errand to run. The fitter had not yet arrived and so I determined to leave the keys under the front doormat for him and write a note regarding any 'specific requirements' as he had put it. I thought hard about this, I really did, but the only thing that suggested itself to my exceedingly practical brain was that Jane is a tad diminutive in stature. The more I thought about this the more it seemed logical to me that the work surfaces would be easier for her to use if they were a fraction lower than normal. I imagined how pleased she would be with this idea of mine, how easily she would be able to glide from surface to surface, baking or washing the dishes etc. So before I left the house I found a notepad and pencil and composed a simple yet succinct message. I put, 'My wife is a small woman'.

Later that day I returned home to find Jane in our new kitchen. I was slightly disappointed that she had arrived before me because I wanted to see the look of rapture on her face when confronted with her customised work surfaces. Her expression was a picture as I walked in but not with the pleasant surprise that I had imagined. She was actually spluttering and speechless with a kind of apoplexy and staring at the floor, or at something very close to the floor. There, about 18' above ground level, our beautiful shiny work surfaces wound around the kitchen, not unlike a motorway as seen from a helicopter. Certainly, they seemed very far away, far down. Jane would have to get on her hands and knees to do any baking. They'd be great for skateboarding perhaps, or conveniently resting your feet whilst cutting your toe-nails.

I wasn't sure how well those suggestions might go down with my better half so, quickly, I did what I could to rescue the situation. 'Well,' I said, 'who on earth would do such a thing? Call him a professional! You should have left it to me after all.'

I don't think I will be getting any home made cakes in the foreseeable future.

Farewell Tour

Towards the end of his life my father-in-law developed dementia and would ramble around the local area in a benign but confused state. Once, we found him fast asleep in somebody's front garden, completely unperturbed, and once he made it to a nearby care home, just in time for breakfast! Perhaps the most unusual and alarming times were those when he decided to take the dog for a walk. When I had first known him Les had been a great hill walker and he introduced me to many a little-known trail, cave and wood in the Derbyshire Dales. He would always have his faithful collie to heel, pointing out her upright, black tail with white tip, which he called 'the white plume of freedom'.

Free he remained until senility came to stay and then that freedom was sadly curtailed. Whenever he tried to buck the trend and continue with his walks disaster was not far behind. On several occasions Les set out to traverse the valley near where he lived. These were always alarming events because he would never tell us he was going, and invariably he ended up at a farm or in the charge of some kindly hiker. Once, a farmer had to call an ambulance after Les complained of chest pains. This couldn't carry on.

The most alarming time came the day he wandered off along the valley and then fell, trying to clamber over a barbed-wire fence. We didn't realise Les had gone on

Idle Thoughts

one of his rambles until we called at his home and found it empty. Setting off in different directions the whole family combed the area until we found the poor chap entangled, distressed and in pain. It looked like he might have broken some ribs and so we had no option but to phone for an ambulance, not for the first time.

In due course the ambulance arrived, bouncing along the rough track above the valley, and then the paramedics baled out and scrambled down to us. Getting Les onto a stretcher was not a problem but carrying him up the path to the ambulance would be, apparently.

'We have to think of our backs,' said one of the ambulance crew, and the others mumbled their agreement. They all stared rather glumly at one another until the one who had spoken added,

'There's nothing else for it, we'll have to get the air ambulance in.'

This was quickly getting out of hand. Don't they charge you thousands of pounds for the air ambulance? Before we knew it they had called for airborne assistance and after that there was indeed 'nothing else for it' except to wait. I reflected, as we all stood around (except for Les who was lying down, getting colder and colder) that I could probably have carried him up to the ambulance on my own, so feather-light he had become in recent months. But we remained under orders and raised no protest.

After some minutes, the noise of an approaching helicopter caused us to look skyward, and sure enough here it was, manoeuvring onto the valley floor, its downdraft whipping the grass and trees into a frenzy. After touchdown, Les and his stretcher was transferred into the aircraft and then, with more frantic whirring, it became airborne again and prepared for, perhaps, its shortest ever rescue, delivering my father-in law to the waiting ambulance in the field just beyond the valley ridge – a distance of about three-hundred metres.

The family, the medics and various onlookers all set off in hot pursuit and scaled the escarpment just in time to see Les being transferred into the land ambulance. All was going to be well and the small crowd clapped and cheered as the helicopter took off and prepared to head back towards base.

That would have been it except for a couple of things. The first was a thought.

'Who was that person with a very expensive-looking camera filming all the proceedings?'

He had jumped out of the helicopter as if he were one of the crew and had fussed about taking shots from various angles. It was almost as if this scene were being filmed for television. In the back of my mind a niggling doubt now presented itself full on, namely

'Doesn't the BBC broadcast some programme called 'Helicopter Heroes' about the feats of the Yorkshire Air Ambulance Service? And was my father-in-law (who was now sitting up and smiling in the land ambulance) shortly to appear in a dramatic rescue on daytime TV?'

I couldn't make up my mind whether this was a good thing or a bad thing but, as it happened, fate was about to deal a blow that ensured the scene would never be played out before an armchair audience. As

Idle Thoughts

the land ambulance set off towards the lane it must have hit a particularly deep pot hole because, all of a sudden, there was a loud bang and the whole vehicle seemed to lift off into the air, as if following the still hovering helicopter. Les must have been launched with it. As it came to earth once more, the ambulance seemed to settle very low to the ground and the crew got out and stared glumly, again.

What had happened, we discovered later, was that the gas suspension unit had caught the side of the pot hole and become punctured, thereby causing an explosion of gas which, in turn, very nearly catapulted the ambulance, 'to infinity and beyond'. It must have been scarcely three minutes before a second ambulance approached, bouncing down the lane, and then gingerly crossed the field. Les's stretcher was brought out of the first one and changed to the new one. He gave us a feeble wave during the transfer. The second ambulance (or third if you count the air ambulance) managed, with caution, to achieve the lane and its relatively smooth surface.

If a helicopter can look shamefaced then ours certainly did as it finally swooped off to its nest, the BBC still on board. This left us with just the crew of number one land ambulance and their sad machine, waiting to be rescued.

Les was cleaned up and checked over at hospital before being released later that day.

My overarching concern now was how much this operation must have cost the NHS and how were we going to prevent it happening again? Also, was there going to be an enormous bill arriving on our doorstep sometime soon? Back at home, Les chuckled rather uncomprehendingly at all our remonstrations and our cajoling him to stay indoors in future. Only when his GP threatened to have him sectioned and removed to a secure place did it finally get through to him that he must not wander off anymore.

No bill came through our letterbox for which we were grateful and I remain proud of the NHS and what it achieved that day. Les didn't stray again. He stayed at home curled up asleep on his settee for the rest of his life, in his dreams no doubt walking the dog up Mam Tor, Ecton Hill and others of his favourite places in the Derbyshire Dales.

Sycamore

Peter Lancaster

Lost in Translation

One of the enduring pleasures of my life has been the fun to be had from misunderstandings, particularly those arising from mishearing, mispronouncing or misunderstanding words. As a teacher I was often confronted by 'schoolboy howlers', where the wrong word had been used in an essay, such as the girl who wrote about her family's visit to Scotland at New Year where, she wrote, they had celebrated 'mahogany'. Then there was the boy who used the word 'apathy' instead of 'empathy' all the way through his essay, which gave it a novel twist.

Sometimes a person's accent can create misunderstanding. We have a friend who lives in the Rossendale valley in Lancashire who, when visiting London, ordered a cork from a bar. Puzzled, the bartender gave her a wine cork. Embarrassed, our friend wandered back to her table, too shy to repeat her request. What she had really wanted was a bottle of that famous Cola, but her Lancashire vowels had let her down.

I say this amuses me, though the consequences of misunderstandings can be very serious, as when, purportedly, the American government misunderstood a message from the Japanese emperor towards the end of WWII. They translated, 'We make no comment' as, 'We hold you in contempt', prompting the decision to drop atomic bombs on Hiroshima and Nagasaki. If true then a simple error resulted in an estimated 150,000 – 250,000 extra deaths; a hideous consequence.

Certainly, the British habit of understatement caused an awful misunderstanding at one engagement during the Korean War, when 600 troops under the command of Brigadier Tom Brodie were confronted with a force of 30,000 Chinese. American headquarters signalled the beleaguered Brigadier asking how bad the situation was, and when he replied that it was, 'a bit sticky', the Americans took this to mean that things were not particularly difficult, and so did not send reinforcements. In due course, the British regiment was overrun.

The bible is a frequent cause of misunderstanding due to dodgy translation. There is a famous statue of Moses by Michaelangelo, which can be viewed in the church of San Pietro in Rome, where he has placed a pair of horns on Moses' head. This comes about due to confusion with the Hebrew word for 'glowing', which is very similar to the word for 'horn'. The St Jerome's Vulgate bible had Moses with horns when really he should have had a halo!

In the book of Joshua the various tribes of Israel and its environs are often described with the suffix '-ites', so - the Israelites, the Kenites, the Sukkites and the Girgashites etcetera. If these weren't amusing enough the translators appear to be overcome with modesty when dealing with the Shittites and refer to them merely as 'the residents of Shittim'.

The mother of another friend of ours, a middle-aged lady of perfect propriety, was at a bible study run by the vicar, where the tribes of the land of Israel were solemnly debated. All went well until the lady next to her turned to her and whispered: 'As for the Gobshites, they live next door to us'. The two respectable matrons were overcome with giggles and had to make a hasty exit.

Idle Thoughts

Douglas Adams and John Lloyd wrote a spoof dictionary called 'The Meaning of Liff', where they took place names of some British towns and village and invested them with additional meanings. They argued that wonderful, evocative place names such as Great Tosson or Stoke Poges deserved more than just to be identifying marks for a geographical location. Here are some they missed.

Offerings to the 'Meaning of Liff'

ACLE (n.) – a little ache.

POYNTON (vb.) – to point lingeringly, as when watching a train go past with no apparent driver.

HIGHER POYNTON (adj. n.) – as for 'Poynton' but more elevated, such as when witnessing an asteroid blazing through the sky

MACCLESFIELD (n.) – farmland belonging to Old Macdonald

BRAMHALL (n.) – large house occupied by one who has made a good living from vampires.

HIGH LANE (adj. n.) – shortened term for the name of any long-winded viaduct e.g. the Thelwell Viaduct

STOCKPORT (n.) – dealer in fortified wines

LIVERPOOL (n.) – type of organ bank

LOWER PEOVER (n.) – complaint of the prostate gland

ALDERLEY EDGE (adj. n.) – suicidal condition for famous Mash actor

KNUTSFORD (n.) – thigh-deep river crossing

DISLEY (vb.) – trying to describe fine rain when inebriated

HEALD GREEN (part.) – gangrene of the ankle

CHOLMONDELEY (adj.) – bad case of flatulence whilst taking a bath

DIGGLE (vb.) – to dig half-heartedly

DELPH (n.) – an expression of surprise at seeing one of the 'little people'

CLITHEROE (vb.) – to plunge down a slippery cliff path

SCARGILL (prop. n.) – Mafiosi fish

WREXHAM (n.) – a destructive pork butcher

ANGLESEY (n.) – Welsh geometry term

CANTERBURY (vb.) – pick fruit on horseback

VANCOUVER (n.) – specialist vacuum for the interior of commercial motor vehicles

ZAMBIA (n. colloq.) – West Country expression for a glass of ale and a ham sandwich

OLDHAM (n.) – elderly pig

ALTRINCHAM (n) – a jobbing tailor

In its shortest manifestation Flash Fiction is only six words long which poses great constraints upon a writer to create a story with development and a resolution.

Flash Fiction

'Looks like war.' (Boom!) 'It's over.'

Baby shoes for sale, never worn.

After the storm the calm, perhaps.

Encyclopaedia for sale - wife knows everything.

I came, I saw, I conquered.

A man, a woman – what next?

Strange Sayings

There's many a cup twixt lip and slip.

The early worm avoids the bird.

Too many cooks spoil the TV viewing schedule.

Jack Sprat could eat no fat; his wife could eat no lean. He will probably live longer than she will.

Don't count your chickens in the supermarket – you'll be sectioned.

If you aim at the stars you might get your shirt wet.

There's plenty of smoke without fire.

The apple doesn't fall far from the tree but it does fall, observed Newton.

You scratch mine and I'll scratch yours.

A stitch in time might be a Black Hole.

Birds and Bee

When Norman Bee vacuumed the carpet, which he did every Tuesday, it was with an energy and thoroughness rarely witnessed in such a routine task. When Norman washed dishes he did it with a purposeful and single-minded attitude, furiously scrubbing them clean before placing them carefully on the draining board. Even when Norman picked his nose it was with a mechanical precision not normally noted in such a self-absorbing, desultory activity. In fact to Norman, all material things were requiring of order and tidiness.

'A place for everything and everything in its place,' was his motto, and he would busy himself with the means of achieving such a target.

By contrast, when he looked for a mate it was with a shy and hesitant gaze over the girls on the bus, at the supermarket or at the comb factory where he worked. This nervousness might have been because Norman had been teased at school about his surname. Girls would walk past him and make a buzzing sound before giggling off to class. Rough boys would ask him if his ears were full of wax – beeswax. He hadn't thought that Bee was such an unusual name – wasn't there a St Bees? Nevertheless, it became the touchstone, or rather the millstone, of his young life.

Probably it was years of such constant rebuffing that now led Norman to dabble in the unknown world (to him) of online dating. He imagined himself to be so small and insignificant in the eyes of the opposite sex that he was reduced to merely gazing, ruefully and longingly, at the profiles (in every sense) of the myriad numbers of available women who seemed to occupy cyber space. The agencies had names like 'Plenty of Fish' or 'Find Romance' but what Norman wanted more than anything was a soul mate: someone to share his life with; to share his hobbies, his leisure time … his bed?

Such thoughts made Norman giddy and he kept clicking off sites before committing himself to send his profile. That is until, one day, he came across a girl that he really liked the sound of, one who really seemed to resonate with him. According to the web she was originally from Spain, although had migrated to Britain many years ago. Her hobbies included dancing (which Norman did in a fairly mechanical, repetitive way) food and drink, and (here was the clincher) flying. Norman loved flying - specifically micro light aircraft. He never felt freer or safer than when his safety belt was clicked shut in the fragile box of a micro light, buzzing his solitary way through the skies.

Her name was Mera Piaster. He somehow screwed up the courage to register his profile online and express an interest in meeting her. And some time down the line here was the result: Norman was standing outside the entrance to a nightclub in the centre of town, called The Hive. 'Appropriate enough for a Bee,' he thought, and smiled grimly. He hoped he would recognise Mera from her photograph and her description of herself on 'Birds and Bees.com'. She looked to be not so very tall but quite shapely, with dark hair and an unusually pale face for a Latin type. Her eyes looked bright and her mouth suggested a wide smile.

Norman clutched a bunch of flowers in clammy hands and shuffled around in random fashion looking hither and thither for an approaching Mera. She surprised him with a light tap on his back and wheeling around Norman found himself staring down at an elegant, attractive woman who introduced herself as Mera Piaster. She smiled as he awkwardly thrust the flowers at her and indeed her smile was wide; so wide that it pulled her nose down, rather hooked, over her top lip. Her eyes, though bright, didn't really smile to match her mouth but Norman was not at all unhappy and they exchanged pleasantries before entering the complex, dark and stifling world of The Hive.

In the refracted light of the club Mera's clothes glistened with exotic colours: a yellow pashmina, blue dress and orange netted tights. Norman couldn't fail to be impressed.

'Very Mediterranean,' he thought.

They danced: he in a bumbling way and she swooping and diving around him – most accomplished. However, it had been many years since Norman had last danced so vigorously and he soon felt out of breath and disorientated. Mera seemed to sense this and she shouted into his ear that they might try somewhere quieter.

'A bar perhaps?'

The Honey Pot was a much better place for conversation. It was one of those rare venues that metamorphose from a tea shop and café by day to a drinks bar at night. Norman and Mera talked formally about this and that until Norman happened to mention micro light aircraft. Mera's bright eyes positively glowed as she animatedly talked about her love of flying and of gliding in particular. She hypnotised Norman with descriptions of soaring high amongst the clouds surveying the world below and the cars that moved like ants along the ground. In Mera's mind even the hang gliders and micro lights wheeled ineffectually far beneath her glide path.

The evening passed quickly and by the end of it Norman felt that he knew Mera as well as anybody since his parents had died. He contemplated asking her back to his flat for a coffee but she pre-empted him by placing an urgent hand on top of his and making a similar offer. Norman's palms felt a little sticky at the thought but he readily agreed and so, a short train journey later, he found himself sitting on a sofa bed in a small but cosy apartment which overlooked the town.

'Welcome to my little nest,' said Mera, her Spanish accent falling like birdsong on Norman's ears. 'Make yourself comfortable, Norman.'

She slipped into the kitchen only to emerge a moment later with two large glasses of wine.

'Oh, I don't really drink,' protested Norman, but Mera waved his protests away before settling next to

Idle Thoughts

him on the sofa bed. 'Don't be silly,' she smiled, 'It is only sweet sherry.'

They talked and drank and then drank and talked, until it seemed to Norman that only he was drinking and talking and Mera looked down upon him intently, as if from a great height. His words started to run together into a continuous, low buzzing sound and Mera's eyes glittered at his every unsteady movement. Suddenly she stood up, as if airborne, and loomed in a dominating way over Norman, her mouth opened wide into a sort of smile.

'Norman Bee.' She pronounced his name with relish. 'Do you know what my name means?'

'What? Mera Piaster?'

'Yes. It is taken from the Latin name for a bird – the European Bee Eater. Now, I wonder if you have a bee-sting. Shall we see?'

After a week or so the police were informed by Norman Bee's landlady that he hadn't been seen for some time, and that she was very worried because it wasn't like him. A cursory examination of his room and computer quickly established his last known movements and his rendezvous with a certain Mera Piaster. It was easy to follow the trail via The Hive and The Honey Pot to Mera's home address, and, when entry had been forced (because of there being no answer) to tell what had probably happened; easy but not nice... not nice at all. There were some clothes scattered about, that forensics later identified as Norman's, but no other trace of him... save a small piece of withered skin on the sofa bed. Perhaps it was

Norman's 'sting', the only part of the bee that the bee eater spits out.

East of Ipswich

You have only to observe the birds in the garden to see that the process of mating and subsequent parenthood is a tiring affair - one that is carried out throughout all creation and not just by Homo sapiens. In the spring the sleek young blackbirds appear like matadors, flashing their yellow beaks and parading up and down the lawn in provocative sallies, pausing from time to time for all to admire them; calling beautifully the while just to emphasise the point. This is all part of the serious business of finding a partner and, when one has been acquired, fending off rivals and setting up a desirable territory in order to secure the deal. The female is often fussy or uninterested, or just playing 'hard to get' until she has found the very best provider and survivor.

Eventually, they form a pair and sing sweetly together of their union, before working hard at building a nest in a suitable tree or hedge. After consummation the female lays her eggs and settles down to hatch them whilst the male has his work cut out collecting worms and grubs for her, as well as fending off cats and other potential dangers.

From morning to night they are busy, but this is as nothing compared to the hard work that begins with the arrival of the baby blackbirds. The little ones demand food, calling incessantly, and both parents, who are now beginning to look a little frayed around the edges, scurry about with full beaks, trying to keep their offspring contented. By the time summer comes the fledglings fly the nest and yet they still trail after the exhausted and frantic adults, squawking greedily to be fed.

Personally, I always found the etiquette of finding a suitable mate quite beyond me. At school, the girls were always so much more mature than me and I didn't really stand a chance with them. Perhaps I was the runt of the litter and Jane only took pity on me when she agreed to be my wife (I'm insecure as well!).

Volumes have been written on the subject of relationships and parenting. Much study and experimentation has been conducted over the best ways to conceive and to give birth. Thereafter, many learned minds have puzzled over the various stages of child development, and countless generations of nurses and nannies have brought their experience to bear. However, we all start as amateurs in the bedroom and everywhere else, rearing our young as best we can, finding out what works by trial and error, the joys and tribulations tumbling after each other in equal numbers.

As I look back over several decades of being a dad it is with a sense of wonder and pride that I see our daughter grown into a confident and successful adult, but demands and cares remain. One friend likened the situation to wheels.

'Bringing up children is all about wheels' he remarked one day. 'They start off with pram wheels and then move onto bicycle wheels and then finally car wheels – it just gets more expensive as you go on.'

Idle Thoughts

Cars are one thing but they are as nothing compared to the expense and demands made by the purchase of a child's first house. Our daughter recently bought a house in the East of Ipswich, as she works in the locality, and Jane and I were dragooned into 'doing up' the place. The house is a modest terrace in an interesting area of town which has a cosmopolitan population. Young professionals rub along with immigrants from all over the world and there are still the older folk who have been there all their lives and pass the odd, dry comment on the changes they see.

'I suppose you think that all this work will be repaid one day?' said one gimlet-eyed old lady who lived opposite to us as we emerged one day blinking in the sunlight, covered in dust and paint. 'I suppose you think that your daughter will look after you when you become old and feeble? Well, children don't! As soon as you start to lose your marbles they'll cut out all the name tags on your clothes, take you to A and E, spin you round three times and then run off.'

She cackled a bit at her pithy comment before going on, 'I believe the woman next door to you makes a lot of noise sexually.'

She said this straightforwardly, casually, as if she were passing a remark about the weather or giving directions into town. Then she turned and walked off leaving Jane and me to stare at one another with shocked, plaster-filled eyes. We had begun to enjoy staying in this little place as it reminded us of our first home but we had forgotten that having party walls can bring consequences.

The first couple of nights after receiving this awkward and bizarre information passed uneventfully, although we were intrigued, if not a trifle anxious about what might happen. The third night however, I was awoken from a deep sleep by a noise that suggested there might be a wounded animal in the garden – a badger perhaps. As I struggled into consciousness my next thought was that the noise (which was a kind of piercing wail) might be one of those old civil defence air raid sirens going off. But why was it being tested in the small hours? The noise went on, its tone rising and falling, occasionally punctuated by a banshee-like screech which suggested nothing less than that the harrowing of hell was taking place somewhere close by.

Finally the penny dropped – the lady next door must be 'entertaining' as it were; and her bedroom was merely a single brick's thickness away from ours. As the blood-curdling sound went on and on my mind was led down some strange, undesirable paths. Whatever the racket I couldn't help but admire the woman's stamina. Maybe she was a 'lady of the night'? But if she were she certainly wouldn't be making much money the length of time she was taking, unless she charged by the hour. Maybe it was a more informal arrangement where regulars just made a donation to a charity of her choice? Enough! I am glad to remain a bit of an amateur. East of Ipswich this might be but definitely East of Eden.

One Shade of Grey
(a tribute to E.L. James)

'These are a few of my favourite things,' said the man, indicating various sculptures, ornaments and pieces of art work that adorned the walls and cabinets of the room.

'They are exquisite,' thought the woman. 'Just imagine - a man of such obvious wealth and refinement inviting me back to his house. Where might this lead?'

The lighting was subdued, just as it h ad been in the bar where they had met for drinks only two hours earlier. But the bar had not had these amazing views over the city.

She sipped the cocktail he had mixed for her and watched him as he talked about the treasures, running his fingers through his thick, dark hair as he did so. 'That's a Lowry, and that's an Epstein.' His voice was casual, bored almost.

'What sort of things do you like?' he asked, suddenly. Was there a hint of suggestion in his voice? He sat down languidly on the long sofa opposite the woman and picked up a remote control from the coffee table between them. He pressed a button and curtains swished silently back on another large window to reveal an enormous patio, painted in the middle with a circle containing the letter 'H'.

'And that's my chopper,' he remarked, with a throwaway gesture. The woman gasped involuntarily as she followed his gaze to a helicopter, parked daintily just beyond the initial focal point.

'No, not that' he said, a note of slight irritation creeping into the suave tones. 'That belongs to my brother. I meant the BMX bike.' There was a little chopper bike leaning against the wall, just to the right of the helicopter. 'I used to compete for Scunthorpe you know.'

'Ah,' she said, trying not to sound disappointed. 'That must have been very challenging.'

'There were some tough calls,' he said. 'There have to be if you want to get to the top.' He pressed another button and the lights brightened. 'Here I am at the 1999 regional championships, in Stoke-on-Trent.' He stood up to point out a photograph of what appeared to be a tangle of BMX bikes and people on the floor. As he did so she noticed that he had a slight limp.

'It was a bad crash. That's where I got the leg. He rolled up his trouser leg slightly and tapped what appeared to be some sort of pot.

'Oh well,' thought the woman, 'you can't have everything. He does have lovely hair.'

'Yes,' he continued, 'and this photo shows the pile up of 2003 in Pontefract. A bloke ran right over my scalp; tore it off completely.'

He abruptly whipped his arm over his head deftly removing a very full wig of hair. His bald scalp shone slightly under the lights. Still she tried not to look shocked. After all he was rich and he did have a flashing smile. He flashed it at her now as he flopped down next to her, picking up his false leg and placing it on the seat cushions. 'Come on,' he teased. 'You haven't told me what you like yet.'

The woman swallowed hard and forced herself into making a provocative comment. 'Well,' she purred, 'I have been known to enjoy having my ears nibbled.

'Blimey,' exclaimed the man, 'I'll need to put my other dentures in for that. These are as blunt as anything.' He reached for the drawer of a nearby cabinet and rummaged around. This was turning into a nightmare. She hung on to the thought that he had to be very wealthy, despite his physical shortcomings. 'It is very good of you to allow your brother to keep his helicopter at your house.'

'What? No, it's not my house, it's his. I hadn't got anywhere to live. There's not much money in BMX you know.' The man seemed to have found his other teeth and gnashed them slightly as he moved along the sofa towards the woman. As he got closer she caught a whiff of body odour mixed uninvitingly with halitosis.

'What I'd really like is to take you upstairs and show you my etchings,' he said.

The woman considered the man dispassionately for the first time and came swiftly to a decision.

'No,' she said. 'Why don't I stay here and you can bring your etchings down?'

Bucket List

As I approached what used to be known as the end of middle age and the beginning of old age, i.e. sixty years old, I decided to create my own 'bucket list'. For those of you not in the swing, a 'bucket list' is a compilation of things that you would like to do before you die; ideally, things out of the ordinary or exotic. It doesn't really mean stuff like getting a good night's sleep or successfully catching next door's cat in the act of messing in your garden. No – a bucket list should consist of things you have always aspired to. They may be things that are difficult to achieve, such as getting yourself into orbit, or they may be idiosyncratic, like doing sword swallowing on top of a flagpole. In my case I couldn't think of anything out of the ordinary that I wanted to do or to have. I am generally a content sort of chap and as long as I receive three square meals a day and maybe a pint of beer, then I am happy.

Nevertheless, worrying that I might be complacent and unfashionable, I scratched my head (which wasn't on the list) and tried to imagine what I really might like to do before my demise. One extremely romantic idea that has floated into my mind from time to time over the years is that of sailing around the Greek Islands. I could just picture myself standing on the deck of a mighty yacht, holding on to the mast and assuming a manly pose whilst scanning the horizon for hazards such as other boats, lobster pots, fish fingers and so on.

Idle Thoughts

The sea and the sky would be a deep azure and the boat would carve its way sleekly through the waves, causing them to part in a creamy white froth. You can see it I'm sure. Other images popped into my head unbidden: adverts from years go - a packet of Consulate menthol cigarettes (cool as a mountain stream) or 'white, white Ultra Brite toothpaste'. Don't ask me why.

This fancy grew over a period of time and I happened to mention it one day to a friend of mine. As it happens, this friend is a newly qualified Yacht Master, or Ocean Wizard or something, a title they give you after you have negotiated the waters of the world with nothing but a rubber dinghy and a ball of string. Immediately he proposed a trip. I assented vaguely but this was all he needed. Before you could say 'shiver my timbers' he had booked a flight to Greece, chartered a boat and the two of us, along with our anxious wives, were on our way. The only trouble was I had to be First Mate.

I was surprised at how easy it all seemed at first. Apparently, all I was needed for was to press a button to lower or raise the automatic anchor. My friend assured me that the boat was high-tech and could practically sail itself. As for the conditions - October on the Ionian Sea promised to be a peaceful and sunny experience. Perfect.

I shopped for sundry items that I thought might possibly of use: a pair of handmade deck shoes (originally priced at £200.00 but fortuitously reduced to £13.99) a linen suit (for cocktails on the poop deck) and a wide brimmed sun hat with chin strap (in case of a sudden gust). Other items suggested themselves: insect repellent, sun tan cream, ear plugs (I don't know why these). Before we knew it we were walking through the metal detector at Manchester Airport and, as usual, there was I setting off the alarm. I had removed my wallet, watch and trouser belt and anything else containing metal, but I had forgotten the small metallic pill box in my jumper pocket (beep-beep-beep).

'Please step this way sir and raise your hands above your head'.

I stood (with my trousers falling down) in the scanner and was no doubt revealed in all my inadequacy to the sniggering customs officers. Nothing was found and so after being frisked and questioned I was allowed to join my embarrassed companions.

Finally, we boarded our plane and my heart leaped along with the aircraft as it roared down the runway, then 'Whee!' up into a blue sky and on our way to the land of Homer, Aristotle and the kebab!

The first big shock about Greece was that you are not able to put toilet paper down the loo but instead you have to put it in a bag at the side of the pan. This option might be popular with flies but it didn't go down well with me and I thought perhaps the philosophers of the School of Athens could have bent their minds to more prosaic issues than polemics or rhetoric. The problem was compounded when it was revealed that we couldn't flush paper down the toilet on the boat either. This made for a pretty stinky prospect as we only moored up once a day. It transpired that the way to get rid of effluent on the boat was to sail a certain

Idle Thoughts

number of miles out and then man the bilge pump. This resulted in a brown slick several hundred yards long seeping from the stern; here's one I did earlier, as it were. Never mind, it was life on the ocean wave.

The briefing by the representative of the boat owner was a rather more unsettling experience. It seemed that pressing the button on the automatic anchor involved rather more than a casual finger flex from the safety of the cockpit. No, first I had to wobble down to the front end of the boat (the bow I believe they call it) and open a hatch, clipping it to the handrail, whilst taking care not to fall overboard.

'Failure to do this will result in considerable discomfort if the hatch falls on you,' grinned the cheerful Australian giving me the demonstration. In fact, he didn't say that, he said,

'It'll bloody hurt mate.'

But he did grin.

Next was the problem of making sure the anchor ascended and descended in a straight line. Dire consequences were to be expected if it came up crooked. This meant that I had to use hand signals to inform the skipper at the back of the boat which way to turn the helm. I could already foresee trouble ahead and, as if the Greek gods were aware of my premonitions, a rumble of thunder rolled down the face of the mountain that fringed the marina. I hardly had time to digest this piece of pathetic fallacy when I found that I was called upon to demonstrate the anchor manoeuvre. The thing is, with your left hand giving signals and your right hand gripping the anchor remote control there was a definite lack of hands with which to hold on to the handrail. Just as well the sea was calm – rumble, rumble.

Let me not be negative. The boat was sleek and lovely, although a tad small. My wife and I were sharing the forward cabin which meant that as the boat narrowed at the bow so did our bed. A quick trial decided us to put our feet to the narrow end rather than our heads as this avoided unwonted bumps, but it meant that to get out of bed you had to swing your feet over your partner, rather like a crane, resulting in undesirable shocks if they happened to wake up at the wrong moment.

My friend was the skipper of the boat and he took his responsibilities seriously, quite rightly. He ran through other duties I had to perform as First Mate if say he fell overboard or was rendered unconscious; how to operate the radio to give a Mayday call, how to launch the emergency dinghy, how to let off flares etcetera – rumble, rumble.

To remember the various nautical terms for parts of the boat I applied what psychologists call a 'stacking system'. This is where you give a more familiar, earthy name to bits of the boat which should then remind you of their technical names. Thus the fenders became for me 'festerings', the Genoa sail the 'Gungeo' and the prow 'the prick'. It didn't work out exactly as I'd hoped, however. I did remember the strange names and could apply them to the parts but I still couldn't give the real name. Therefore it was the skipper who had to change. Any passing boat might be astonished at hearing commands such as

Idle Thoughts

'Attend the barnacle' (binnacle) or 'Roof the mainsail' (reef) and 'Cast off the prick'.

When this extended into the realm of ordering Greek food the skipper put his foot down

'I am not going to call a Lamb Kleftiko a Lamb Kalashnikov' he grumbled.

When we left Manchester the weather had been fine but Greece seemed to have acquired some of the UK's customary gloom. The sky was leaden as we set sail on the first day, though I felt like Odysseus slipping from our moorings and embarking on a great... well... odyssey. Nor did we leave alone. Another friend of our skipper was taking a boat for the first time, and as crew he had acquired a group of blokes with very varying degrees of sailing experience. They quickly became known to us as the Pirates of the Caribbean, particularly after their first attempt to park (moor up) when they spent three hours circling around the harbour issuing a steady and colourful stream of expletives. They somehow managed to lose their anchor, set two men adrift in a dinghy and, at one stage, see the skipper abandon ship in a brave but potentially dangerous attempt to rescue the dinghy.

Their equivalent of Jack Sparrow further introduced himself later when, after an evening spent at a local taverna, he sat on the top deck of his boat and proceeded to play a CD of 'Werewolves Over London' by The Grateful Dead, at full volume. After a few moments there came a rapping on the hull and a posh, English voice said,

'Would you turn off that noise, there are other people in this harbour as well as you.'

'Go forth and multiply' (or words to that effect) responded Jack.

The request was repeated, incurring the same response and then a voice, as equally Home Counties as the first, drifted across from the other side of the harbour:

'They're from the North, you know.'

The next morning, well and truly put in our place as plebs and barbarians, we negotiated the harbour entrance and set sail for our destination – Krapos (as all the Greek Islands came to be called, due to their drainage arrangements)

One of the endearing yet infuriating characteristics of the Greek islanders is their easy-going attitude to life. When the Greek met office languidly announced that the wind was to be only force 1-2, a gentle breeze and the weather 'scorchio', I had looked forward to a very pleasant day's sailing, deserving of a big tick on my bucket list. What we got was Force Six and Seven gales and a wind speed of thirty knots plus. To give you some idea of what this means imagine being on a giant roller coaster for four hours, with your seat not only going up and down but also corkscrewing wildly, and every so often a bathtubfull of water comes hurtling over the side and over your head. The sea became mountainous and my wife kept shifting constantly in my line of vision. Sometimes she would be directly below me and then, after a violent lurch by the boat, she would be above me. At all times she was clinging on for dear life and something told me that when I had sold her this trip it wasn't with the idea of such a terrifying dance with death.

Our skipper remained implacable, however, and merely murmured that perhaps it was time for life jackets and safety harnesses. As first mate it was my duty to get these items from down below and so I set off as best I could. Those occasions in my life when I have had too much to drink came to mind now. The floor seemed to change its angle constantly and it was all I could do to struggle back on deck with the gear without suffering severe concussion. The pots crashed wildly in the cupboards and the toilet slopped revoltingly in the bathroom.

Putting on the safety equipment was like a rather deadly pantomime but eventually we all ended up strapped to something. I retain only the greatest admiration for our skipper, who never lost his nerve and remained reassuringly calm throughout. Whilst the rest of us were variously screaming, knocking ourselves out or being ill, he calmly manned the helm and navigated us out of danger, into a sheltered mooring. God bless him.

That first day was a baptism of fire but we didn't have the like again for the rest of the week. Yes, there was always the irritating attitude of those already moored up as we crashed and lurched and panicked our way into our berth. They were so smug! Surely, everybody has to learn? There were the other characters we bumped into (sometimes literally) such as Bareback Barry or Itchy and Scratchy, the scrofulous restaurateurs. There was Fat boy Slim and his so-solid crew, who could eat and drink without a break for hours on end. They even stopped for a round of sandwiches in the middle of casting off.

Altogether it was a memorable trip, perhaps an expedition rather than a holiday. When I had originally put it on my bucket list I little realised that I would come quite close to kicking the bucket, or at least being sick in it.

Idle Thoughts

This ditty was inspired by the modern driver.

The Wacky Races

(To the tune of The Hokey Cokey)

You put your right foot down,
Your right foot up,
Foot down on the gas,
So no one else can pass.
You do the Wacky Races,
And you don't slow down,
That's what it's all about.

(chorus}
Oh, do the Wacky Races!
Oh, do the Wacky Races!
Oh, do the Wacky Races!
That's what it's all about.

You fail to indicate,
Or very, very late,
Round about the roundabout,
And don't forget to shout.
You do the Wacky Races,
And you don't slow down,
That's what it's all about.

(chorus)
Oh, do the Wacky Races! ... etc.

Peter Lancaster

You get your mobile out,
And then you start to spout,
Flash your lights and blast your horn,
And shake the car about.
You do the Wacky Races,
And you don't slow down,
That's what it's all about.

(chorus)
Oh, do the Wacky Races! ... etc.

You put your right fist up,
Your right fist down,
Fist up, fist down,
Making sure you frown.
You do the Wacky Races,
And you don't slow down,
That's what it's all about.
(chorus)

Oh, do the Wacky Races! ... etc

Idle Thoughts

Skimmer Frame

Face Book

Did you look?
Did you look?
What did we do before Face book?
Well me, I stared at the wall,
Happily, happily.

Hear the gossip,
Dish the dirt.
Katie Price in Peter's shirt?
Celebrities,
Shoot the breeze,
Kim on Twitter,
Did Kanye hit her?

 (chorus)
Did you look? ...etcetera

Loads of pictures,
That's my life,
Here's one of me,
With someone's wife.
There's one of what,
I had for tea,
And one when I just had to wee.
Here's another,
Of my pet,
And one I'd rather just forget.

 (chorus)
Did you look? ...etcetera

Idle Thoughts

I'm not nosey,
I'm quite sweet,
But have you seen what's on her feet?
This is us in Timbuktu,
If you don't like it,
Face book you!

Peter Lancaster

Going Downhill Fast

When God ordained that we should age,
Because of Adam's fall,
I never thought that it would mean,
I wouldn't stand so tall.

I seem to shrink with passing days,
Most hobbit-like I grow,
The kids on fertiliser feed,
To them the ceiling's low.

I never knew my lovely hair,
All golden-brown and wavy,
Would turn quite grey and then fall out,
To end up in the gravy.

My strong, white teeth are yellowing,
All gapped like battlements,
At night my false ones grin at me,
From a glass of Steradent.

False hips, false knees, whatever next?
I'm going to be a rebel.
I'll buy a brand new motorbike,
And a leather suit in purple.

I'll roar at ninety miles an hour,
Up narrow country lanes,
And shout abuse at passers-by,
Till I forget my pains.

Idle Thoughts

I'll eat pork pies and sweets and chips,
And drink the strongest liquor,
I'll make rude noises from the pew,
And aim them at the vicar.

I'll lie in bed and vegetate,
A couch potato I,
Become a pensioned teenager,
Giving girls the eye.

Oh no, this surely cannot be,
The world I cannot sully.
Dear Lord, help me accept my lot,
And grow old gracefully.

Goldie

Fairytales and Scapegoats

'Do you believe in fairies? If you believe, clap your hands.'

So says Peter Pan, towards the end of the play by J.M. Barrie. The appeal is made in order to revive the dying fairy, Tinker Bell, who has deliberately taken some poison intended for Peter in order to save his life. If she dies he won't; she is sacrificing herself for him. At the first ever performance, a hush fell as the young audience digested this urgent request, and then they began to clap and clap, louder and faster, until the actor playing Tinker Bell leapt into life again. The audience had awakened its faith.

A similar scenario is enacted in Shakespeare's 'A Winter's Tale' when Leontes, after sixteen years of regret and repentance for jealously banishing Hermione, his innocent wife, is shown a 'statue' of her by a faithful servant. The audience can see that the statue is actually Hermione, but they accept that Leontes cannot see what is all too apparent to them. They suspend their disbelief as the servant enjoins Leontes,

'It is requir'd you do awake your faith'.

The 'statue' of Hermione then comes back to life and steps down from the plinth, to embrace her tearful husband. This is Shakespeare's great play about sacrifice and resurrection, and it is a theme reworked again and again in literature, from Sleeping Beauty to Harry Potter.

The Oxford academics and writers C.S. Lewis and J.R.R. Tolkien were great believers in what they called 'true myths' i.e. they believed that stories of sacrifice, substitution for wrongs, and resurrection from the dead (stories common to many ancient cultures) are true in the sense that although they pre-date Christianity they prefigure it and point to the truth of it. They argued that in such storytelling man becomes a sub-creator after God (the great Creator) because we have, in-built, God's nature: a sense of right and wrong and of justice, a sense of morality and personal responsibility. Thus, 'The Lion, the Witch and the Wardrobe' and 'The Lord of the Rings' play out the struggle between good and evil according to Christian beliefs.

Interestingly, the more anyone explains to me Einstein's Law of General Relativity the more the idea of parallel universes seems likely; a spirit world may well be out there in some sense. Ghost stories, premonitions and intimations of immortality may not be completely fanciful – they might just be scientific.

Christians believe that Jesus actually existed and that the bible accounts are true. He was fully human and yet fully God. His sacrifice opens the way for all. He is the only one who has the authority to right our wrongdoing, make up for our shortcomings, heal our hurts and bitterness; in essence to make us the sort of persons we were meant to be, and in our better moments wish to be!

The Jewish faith required that a goat without blemish be driven into the wilderness to die, as a substitution for the sins of the people. The Christian says, 'At last, no more scapegoats!'

Here Endeth...

If we think about the way we use the term 'faith' in our society, various examples readily come to mind: we may belong to a 'faith', by which we mean a religion, or we might swear to be faithful to our future partner if we are getting married. We must surely have faith in the pilot of an aeroplane we travel in or the engineers of a bridge we cross. We trust that the pilot will not crash the plane or that the bridge will not collapse. We employ faith in a whole range of different spheres, both material and spiritual.

One source describes faith as: 'being sure of what we hope for and certain of what we do not see'.

And Jesus is quoted as saying, 'Blessed are those who have not seen and yet have believed', placing a huge emphasis on the importance of having faith. But why should faith be considered to be such a vital quality and does it matter what we have faith *in* so long as we have it? We might say does it matter what we believe in as long as we believe something. Is Santa Claus better than the Tooth Fairy?

During the 1930s many Germans put their faith in Hitler and all that meant: eugenics, genocide and the rest. Were they right? Most would say not. So what we have faith *in* does matter and it is our choice whether we have faith in God. We are told that God loves us as a good father does; that he wants us to put out our little hand and let him take hold of it. But we have free will. God can't or won't force us to love him. If we remain sulky children who won't be helped then he has no other choice than to let us go our own way, wherever we may end up.

This is a Christian viewpoint I know: the idea that faith is a matter of choice. Some might say 'why doesn't God *make* us believe in him? Why doesn't he appear physically, sort out all the ills of the world and then we will believe?'

There was a tongue-in-cheek saying doing the rounds a few years ago that said 'Jesus is coming – look busy!' Do we really think he will be impressed with our busyness when he returns? Do we think that we can pull the wool over his eyes?

I think that God is at work in the world to remedy wrong and to defeat evil - that is his aim; to fit us for that meeting with him one day, face to face. Jesus described himself as God's final word to mankind; accept or reject him; sheep or goat; that is your choice, by faith.

Peter Lancaster

The Language of God

If only you would make it clear,
Banish doubt and guilt and fear,
Magic this and that away,
Stop my hair from turning grey.

Would it be so hard to make me rich?
Satisfy a nagging itch?
Jump off the pages of the Bible,
Indulge me when I'm being idle.

If only you would give a sign,
Turn this orange juice to wine,
Make the sun shine every day,
Agree with everything I say.

Keep me happy all the time,
Help the poor (then they'll be fine),
Exchange my car from red to blue,
Would that be just too much to do?

What's that? It's not supposed to be,
Ugly, crippled, slovenly,
Nothing's quite like what was meant,
People getting old and bent.

Nasty things that sting and bite,
Nations spoiling for a fight,
Couldn't you just wave your arm?
Stop the evil causing harm?

Idle Thoughts

But all I get is that old cross,
Where you suffered pain and loss,
Hanging just above the altar,
Where all come to kneel or falter.

The sculptor manages to trace,
The agony upon your face,
Showing that it was for me,
That you hung there awfully.

There was no other good enough,
To fit us for a life above,
No other way to right the wrong,
Put things back where they belong.

I'm sorry but I can't accept it,
Your creation is decrepit,
I am not able to believe,
Your fairy tales, they just deceive.

I prefer the scientific,
Richard Dawkins is terrific,
On the whole I've made my choice,
I cannot give to faith a voice.

But up ahead I sometimes fear,
Time's departure lounge draws near,
This choice I hope I will not rue,
Don't say it's me you never knew.

FAIRY TALES

Faith and Fairy Tales

Fairy ->

    an imaginary very small creature with magic powers; after an old word 'fay' or 'fey', from 'The Fates' - three goddesses who were believed to control people's lives.

Tale ->

    a story.

Story ->

    from the Latin 'historia' meaning history; an account of a real or imaginary event.

History ->

    what happened in the past; learning or finding out.

Findings ->

    the conclusions reached from an investigation.

Investigation ->

    a systematic inquiry.

Inquiry ->

    a close examination of a matter; a search for information or truth.

Truth ->

> representing what has really happened or exists; genuine or proper; loyal and faithful; not false.

Pontius Pilate asked ->

> 'What is truth?'

Jesus said ->

> 'I am the truth.'

Fateful

You sometimes hear people say 'I don't believe in God but I believe in 'Fate'.

Really...?

The Fates were three Ancient Greek goddesses who were supposed to control people's lives; nebulous, random, even capricious characters who acted on a whim. Do people choose to trust in fate rather than in God?

A British soldier, lately returned from Afghanistan, told how he had observed some Afghans being trained by the British to swim carrying a full pack, weighing more than fifty pounds. The sergeant dived into a large tank of water and demonstrated the survival technique. When it came time for the locals to try the first one jumped in, fully equipped, and sank like a stone to the bottom where he lay, completely still; and would probably have drowned had not the sergeant jumped in and hauled him out. When he was asked why he had made no attempt to save himself he replied to the effect that if he was meant to drown then he would drown. The fact that the sergeant jumped in to rescue him, he said, meant that he was not intended to drown.

I am afraid that I would not be content with such a fatalistic philosophy.

Peter Lancaster

Many scientists and philosophers, far from being atheists, have had an active faith in God. Here are a few...

The Scientists Roll of Faith

Galileo, Galileo!
You've got Copernicus, Bacon, Descartes, Newton,
Boyle and Faraday went to church on Sunday.
Kepler, Kelvin always kept their faith in,
Einstein and Planck were always very frank.
Lovell, Rutherford never did forget God.
Old Blaise Pascal, not a dirty rascal,
Boyd and Filho followed Galileo.

Galileo, Galileo!
You've got...
Bede the venerable, he was very stable,
Alister Mc Grath gives us all a laugh
(When he slaughters Richard Dawkins).
St Augustine, Locke and Justin,
Dostoevsky was a clever Ruski,
Solzhenitsyn , Tolstoy and Hopkins,
John-Jacques Rousseau rhymes with Galileo,

Galileo, Galileo!
Milton, Kung and old John Donne,
Soren Kierkegaard (he thought very hard),
Tolkien and Lewis (he's my hero),
Rhymes with Galileo,
Galileo, Galileo!
Galileo, Figaro.
I'm just a poor boy from a poor family.

Idle Thoughts

This is a short story inspired by the sight of an old lady peering from behind some shutters above a taverna in Greece.

Resolution

First there is the heat: relentless, dry heat from the cruel eye in the sky. The eye burns up everything in the plateia - the flowers in the hanging baskets, the water in the little fountain with the statue. It bears down upon the midday shoppers, burning their olive skin, hair and even their eyes, until they flop down under the bleached umbrellas of cafes that crouch on the edges of the square. The heat burns the tables and chairs of the cafes, bakes the stones on which they stand, and flings its glance angrily at the whitewashed buildings; their shutters close like eyelids.

Complicit with the heat – dust clouds; whirling like drunken genies, hurling grit and litter into faces, so that people shrink away into corners to sit out the anger of the Greek gods of summer. They cover their coffee cups and wrestle with newspapers, smoking and talking; baking like pita bread.

It is Sunday and families are out in their best clothes. There is the priest, in full black regalia and beard. He hurries to the nearby church nodding at the café dwellers; anxious to be out of the hot spotlight. He clutches at a black bible.

There also are the café owners, perching uncomfortably on stools by the doors, running sweaty fingers through lank, damp hair; wiping them on greasy aprons and hoping that they won't be called out into the frying pan of the square.

Only the children seem unaware of the heat. They laugh and play, chasing in and out of the tables, some carrying balloons on strings; children of the dust jinn.

Unexpectedly, there is also watchfulness: shutters on a window above a café open slightly, and a small child playing out in the heat and light stops momentarily, her attention caught. The faded, red balloon that had been in her hand drifts upwards towards the window and she catches the merest glimpse of fiery, bright eyes behind the shutter, fiercely reflecting the sun; then gone.

The child resumes the chase, pursuing the balloon now kidnapped by the wind and teasingly circling the square, just out of reach. As the children move about so the eyes reappear and follow them urgently in their game, marking their course amongst the tables with the parents, and round the little statue. When the eyes come to rest upon the statue they narrow and withdraw slightly into the shadows of the upstairs room.

Occasionally a child falls, bangs a knee and starts to cry. The eyes emerge a little more, as if paying close attention and the outline of a woman's head can be made out, covered by a headscarf. A child is caught by a devilish gust and almost thrown into the path of a van travelling up the street. The shutter creaks and briefly there is the face of an old woman behind the fierce eyes, sharp, pinched and brown as a raisin. A mother moves suddenly, strange against the languid backdrop, and snatches the child from danger; her eyes flit to the shuttered window above.

The crying child is seated on the plinth of the statue and grazed knees are cleaned and salved. The mother talks to her daughter and points at the statue. It is of a little girl called Kalika, about the same age as the child, remembered for the time she was sacrificed to the sun god by the dust jinn; blown unmercifully under the wheels of a van. The statue stands to remind the unwary of the dangers nearby. Some thirty years earlier Kalika's mother had placed it there, and still each day she looks from behind upstairs shutters, for the safe-keeping of successive generations.

Lastly, the eyes withdraw, perhaps with some sense of resolution.

Shoddy Goods

Elliott Goode was sitting on one of the velour pull-down seats of the little theatre. He had a thin face with a permanently furtive expression which made him seem to do everything out of the side of his mouth. When he looked at you he turned his head sideways, and when he spoke it was never quite head on, as though he were speaking into some lapel microphone or whispering a state secret. Perhaps he was worried by stalkers, or he had been bullied at school; however, you always felt conspiratorial when conversing with him.

Elliott had a goatee beard and thinning sandy-coloured hair that would have made him look a little like Shakespeare except for the thin face, and so the resultant look was closer to Guy Fawkes. Possibly that accounted for his conspiratorial air. He smoked constantly, guiltily blowing the smoke to the right and the left.

Elliott was currently leading a rehearsal of a bedroom farce by the local amateur dramatic association on the small proscenium stage of the theatre.

The theatre stood on the outskirts of the town, that had grown up and had its heyday in the latter part of the 19th century. It owed its existence to textiles, mainly Shoddy and Mungo, and the subsequent modest prosperity it enjoyed enabled the construction of some fine civic buildings - the little theatre being one of them.

The descendants of those entrepreneurs who had developed the Shoddy and Mungo Works were sufficiently well-heeled to afford the leisure of indulging their thespian aspirations. Sleek cars embellished the theatre's car park and the actresses were accoutred in the latest designer gear. One of them, very well coiffured, was rummaging through her handbag as she listened impatiently to Elliott berating her, slyly, for failing to adopt some particular pose.

'Sylvia, darling, you are wonderful of course,' said Elliott to the seat at his side, 'but I would like you to move more slowly into position.'

The coiffured actress didn't seem best pleased at being criticised and she tutted before moving to where Elliott was indicating.

'Wonderful, but if you could avoid turning to the back wall, darling; you know you shouldn't have your back to the audience.' This said in his usual roundabout way made several other members of the cast shift uncomfortably so that they all ended up facing front.

'Now it looks like a line of bloody dummies' said Elliott irritably to the prompter sitting at the end of his row. 'Make your lines interesting please.'

The cast tried to make themselves visually interesting. One placed a foot on the ottoman at the back of the stage and another contemplated a spot of paint on a flat. The coiffure with the handbag sat heavily on a chair and glowered at Elliott.

'Not on the chair' said Elliott. 'You know that sitting down on stage is boring.'

The actress sprang from the chair and fixed Elliott with a hard stare. Not reading the signs very well Elliott asked them to continue: 'From the top please.'

'From me do you mean?' asked a glum, rather wooden young man.

'Yes.'

'From the ironing board?'

'Yes.'

The wooden young man grappled with his script and the ironing board at his side. The script fell on the floor.

'Sorry, it's ... er...difficult to manage both.'

'Oh, for goodness sake!' (This from the coiffure) 'I might just as well deliver my lines to the ironing board.'

The wooden young man looked embarrassed and managed to grip his script and the ironing board but, unfortunately, this included the release handle for the legs so the ironing board started to extend, squeakily. The young man confusedly tried to speak his line but his hold on the board was tenuous and its scissor legs closed on his fingers.

'Ah! Ow!' he said.

Elliott looked up at the side of the ceiling. 'Just carry on Sylvia.'

Idle Thoughts

The coiffure glowered at the wooden young man and at Elliott, and at everybody else.

'How can I work like this?' she complained. Nevertheless she started with her lines, delivering them all at breakneck speed and with an intonation that suggested she might soon commit murder.

By this time the wooden young man had managed to fix the ironing board at knee height, leaving him both hands to handle his script, and when the coiffure decelerated and came to a halt he paused, whether for effect it was difficult to say, before reading his next line. He might just as well have been reading the telephone directory or the instructions on a flat-pack cupboard for the entire nuance he managed; he was definitely not the 'yang' to coiffure's 'ying'.

Elliott groaned inwardly.

'Prior to this production' he thought, 'the quickest way to empty the theatre would have been to yell fire!'

As soon as the ironing board had completed its lines coiffure was off again, her words machine gunning round the stage until Elliott simply had to intervene.

'Sylvia, darling could you please go slower?'

Off she went once more, like a demented typewriter in danger of meltdown.

'No,' remonstrated Elliott, appealing to the side wall, 'go slower, slower.'

The coiffure was incensed. She stood up and bellowed with all the volume necessary to be heard over the noise of a Shoddy and Mungo works:

'Slower, slower?' she screeched at Elliott. 'It was faster, faster all last night wasn't it, darling?'

And with that she threw down her script and flounced off stage.

Electrocuted or frozen, for once Elliott stared straight forward, whilst it was the turn of everybody else to glance sideways.

Forget Me Not

Morning sun,
Warm and young,
Spring-tickles up the shoots
From frozen earth,
Like hard, dry bone,
Galvanizing withered roots.

Flowers blink,
Then stretch and smile,
Fomenting colour riots.
And buttercups,
Clash gorgeously with
Purple-headed violets.

Deadened hedgerows,
Solemn, drab,
Propriety forget,
Blush with orange poppy heads,
And daisy coronets.
(Which join the progress of a breeze,
Floating gently busy bees.)

This merely though
A prelude to
The busting, splashing
Force of Spring,
Pouting, shouting,
Nature spouting,
All the rules of Winter flouting.

Grasses waving,
Orchestrating,
Whole shebang erupting,
Forget-me-notsing,
Snap-crackle-popsing,
(Hillsides shaking shaggy locks
Of May and dandelion clocks),
Shouts 'Boo' to shades,
Then whispers sweet
Of some green glade,
Some happy place,
Heartsease-in-fragrance,
Herb of grace.

Time past and future both converging
In eternal now,
Lifts up the veil of shadow, curse.
(Dispense with this,
My hapless verse),
No blind watch maker this,
But Love's firm kiss.
A rainbow waterfall
His heart.
Forget Me Not.

Impulse

The A57 was particularly busy. Every morning commuters would join the traffic jam that trailed dispiritingly through the village. They inched forward fretfully in their cars. Some took the opportunity to look at their hair in the rear view mirror, or apply make-up. Some fiddled with the stereo, texted friends or family; and some even ate a breakfast.

When there were road works (which was quite often) the queues became longer and more entrenched, and that's when irritability could spill over into anger. On impulse people would suddenly veer left past a no entry sign to take a short cut through the estate. Having made the decision to infringe the Highway Code, they frequently speeded up to get through as quickly as they could. In an area that had a 30mph speed limit (reducing to 20mph by the school) they sometimes roared by at 40 or even 50 miles per hour. It was as if some residual guilt had to be overcome by flying along as fast as they could.

David Moore was no exception to this rule. Most often, on the way to work, he would try the rat run on impulse, haring past kiddies crossing the road or riding their bikes in a slightly wobbly way. It didn't matter - he could put the danger signals out of his mind. As long as he made a minute on his commute time it was worth it; he would be suffused in feelings of excitement and a sense of achievement.

David was a typical commuter. He worked in an office in the city, and travelled to and fro every day from his semi-detached house on the outskirts of a dormitory town. He was thirty-five, married with one child, and he was engaged in climbing to the top of the 'greasy pole' of his IT company. This meant that he spent a great deal of time planning his next move. Would so and so leave? Would he be better to ignore so and so and cosy up to someone else? Even when he was driving these sorts of thoughts filled his brain.

David was not just a typical commuter, he was typical in the beliefs he held. The spirit of the age had very much taken over his heart. There was some faint belief that there might be a God or life force behind things, particularly pleasant to indulge when looking at a nice sunset or when holding a baby, but this sentimental view had been largely superseded by vague, quasi-scientific notions about psychology, relative values and the Big Bang Theory. It was a cross between, 'Do what you like but don't hurt people (unless they get in your way)', and 'What does it matter in the end anyway because we're all going to die?' and 'What odds can I get for the 3.30 at Epsom?' with, 'If there is a God I am sure that he will see that on balance I am a really nice bloke who can tell him a thing or two about the way it is'.

Never for a minute did David Moore suspect that there might be such a thing as a spirit world, a world of good and evil, of forces that were doing battle for his immortal soul. Never did he dream that the impulses that came to him so frequently were often suggestions from creatures outside himself; that impulse to follow the line of least resistance, 'Do what you want to'. 'Look after number one'. 'Don't take the rap'. 'Don't 'come clean''. 'Cut through the estate... no-one is watching'.

He would have plenty time to think about such matters from his prison cell, and perhaps that would stop the terrifying memory of a child running in front of his speeding vehicle that day.

Desperate Times

The big man swallowed a final mouthful of pie and then wiped the back of his hand over his stubbly chin. He picked up the paper and settled back in his rocking chair to catch up with the news. Crossing his legs as far as his massive thighs and calves would allow he rested the paper on one side of a large boot.

'Price of beef is up again,' noted the man. 'That will affect my food bill.'

As was his custom he quickly turned to the small ads and began scouring the jobs page.

'Not much call for my kind of work these days,' he muttered ruefully; 'too many tractors and fences. Plus, the EU has brought in masses of rules and regulations.'

He mentally crossed off jobs he had tried but failed: door security for example. It had not worked out because he couldn't ever decide who to let in and who not to. His good nature had made him an easy touch for potential troublemakers. 'But don't let them get me mad,' he said to himself. That's why he had got the sack. He had lost his temper and punched a bloke through a wall.

And then there was always the problem of Dawg. His pet mutt always had to go where he went otherwise it would howl all day long.

Idle Thoughts

Most of the jobs in The Times seemed to be for IT experts or Media Consultants. A man couldn't get his teeth into a job like that. 'No,' there was no way round it; if he was to avoid the humiliation of starvation then drastic action was called for. He patted his trusty revolver in the holster at his side. At least the police hadn't managed to get that off him yet.

'This world ain't no place for an old cow poke like me, Dawg,' the man said as he poured himself another double-double measure of bourbon. He could just picture the headlines in tomorrow's paper – 'Dan shoots himself whilst balance of mind affected. Surely now gun law must be rigorously enforced?' It would be a case of 'Desperate Times calls for desperate measures.'

Chocolate

I am sure that at the end of time when we are all called to account I am going to be viewed as a sanctimonious hypocrite. 'Oh, don't be so hard on yourself,' I hear you chide, most charitably, and it is very sweet of you to say so but no... I fear I deserve what I will get.

Take the matter of chocolate, for example. Now I am not a great addict of chocolate, being able take it or leave it according to whim but there are those (is it mainly the female of the species?) that it seems cannot do without it. As well as merely eating chocolate they seem to talk about it all the time; dream about it, fantasise about it – I kid you not. They ingest chocolate as a pick-me-up or as a calm-me-down, as a reward, a prize, a satiate and as a panacea for all life's ills.

Whether it be chocolate orange, plain, milk or mocha; truffle, flake or fondue, chocolate is, for some people, the ubiquitous answer. Wars may be fought over it or ended by it, relationships broken or cemented by it, work relieved, energy restored, desires indulged.

You think I exaggerate? You think I am talking as if I were slightly unhinged, in need of some chocolate perhaps? Well let me tell you the story of a personal domestic tragedy, admittedly of a relatively trivial nature, and you can judge for yourselves where I stand in the cosmic scales of justice.

My dear wife, may I say a paragon of wifely accomplishments, approached me one day wearing a new dress and asked me, innocently enough, if this particular garment made her bottom look big. There is of course no safe answer to this question and whilst I weighed carefully the various options open to me I noticed a box of chocolates open on a table nearby. My mind was immediately possessed with smug and pompous homilies and I blithely replied, 'No dear, it was all the chocolate you ate that did that.'

The story, and indeed my life, might have ended at this point but, gracious lady that she is, my wife merely smiled, perhaps a little thinly, and responded 'Take care my love; remember that pride cometh before a fall,' and we both laughed heartily at the joke.

Time passed without a care and then one day I received a phone call from a friend who had just moved to Colwyn Bay for his health. He informed me that the people he had bought his new house from had emigrated and that as such were unable to take many of their cherished goods with them including, lounging in the garage, a classic Jaguar motor car, which came with the house. My friend found it surplus to his requirements and wondered whether I might be interested in purchasing it (for a laughably low price.)

Now as it happens, I may not have a soft spot for chocolate but I do have one for classic motor cars and found myself practically salivating down the telephone at the thought of owning such a beast as a Jaguar. After suitable negotiations and the usual tiresome administrative necessities I eventually found myself travelling by train to Colwyn Bay in order to collect my gleaming big cat. What a thrill to take possession of such a beast and drive it back to High Lane. What a growling noise from the V8 engine; what a purring noise from me as I whisked past lesser vehicles. In no time I was home and now there she was on the drive, complete with private number plate, for all the neighbours to envy. 'Look upon my works ye mighty, and despair'.

All was well for a day or two with me instituting a rigorous polishing regime and smiling a tad patronisingly at all who passed by. Then came that Sunday ... I had been to see a friend in the jag, who was suitably impressed with it, and then arriving home I attempted to effect a befitting nonchalant turn into our drive. Suddenly there was this most awful scraping noise as the front wing of my pride and joy caught the bolt on our driveway gates. My rich grin turned to one of horror as I leapt out to inspect the damage and there, dark and ugly as sin, I discovered a four inch dent in the bumper and paintwork scraped, revealing a jagged scar. To say I was aggrieved would not be an understatement - it would be a statement from a different planet; I was mortified, incendiary, scandalised; spitting not feathers but whole chickens. I fled, wounded into the house before I lost my dignity and collapsed in a frothing, howling heap on the carpet.

Some time after this (minutes, hours, days?) I thought that it was all out of my system and dragged myself to my feet where, head erect, I progressed in a controlled sort of fashion into the kitchen to make myself a cup of the brew that cheers. Calm now I prepared cup and saucer, milk and tea-bag and was just reaching for the kettle when I realised that it was exactly the same colour as my precious car, a fact that had never occurred to me before. Overcome by some black surge of resentment and fury at the nature of the universe I slammed the kettle down onto its stand where, happy to accept and obey the universal laws of nature, it promptly snapped in half under the effects of the unusual forces applied to it. Watching this disintegration as if in slow motion my brain promptly prepared to commit a similar sort of hara-kiri and I realised that to prevent such a thing I must get out of the house immediately.

Rushing out into the street I ran pell-mell to our local shop. We needed some milk and it was a good excuse to get out. Miserably sliding the two litre container out of the fridge I did something I have never done before ... I dropped it. The milk slipped out of my hand, descended to the floor and, with a dreary slopping sound, split open, spilling its contents generously on the shop floor.

I was told afterwards that they were very good with me. They mopped up the milk, didn't charge me for it and instead, later, were only too happy to sell me their entire stock of chocolate.

Peter Lancaster

This is for people who get tied up with regulations.

On the Seventh Day

Play opening sequence of God Shuffled His Feet by the Crash Test Dummies – up to the end of verse one.

Voice: After six days He was quite tired so God said 'Let there be a day for picnics with wine and bread'. He gathered up some people He had made, created blankets and places in the shade.

Birdsong. Lights up to reveal people sitting on blankets, sipping wine and eating bread. After a few moments 'A' begins to look frustrated.

A: Excuse me. *pause.* I said excuse me.

B: Shhh.

A: Sorry, I only said excuse me.

B: I'm not sure we're allowed to …

A: I only wanted to know if I could stretch my legs a bit.

B: Stretch your legs.

A: Yes - go for a walk or a run.

B: *Sucking in breath.* Well I think I would have to consult on that one.

A: Consult who?

Idle Thoughts

B: The others ... over there. *He indicates a couple on another blanket.*

A: Alright.

B: All right what?

A: Alright, consult the others.

B: Oh. Alright. *He clears his throat to attract the attention of C and D.*

C: Shhh.

B: Excuse me.

C: What?

B: Sorry. It's just that our colleague here wants to know if he can go for a walk.

D: Go for a walk ...?

B: Or a run.

C: A run!

A: Well, did God say that we couldn't go for a run?

D: He told us to drink wine and sit on blankets.

C: So that is what we are doing.

D: Happily.

C: Fervently.

B: Quite... so there. Be satisfied.

A: I suppose, *pause. They all sip wine simultaneously* but...

B: What now?

A: I was just wondering, could I play some music?

B: Did God specifically state we could play music?

A: Well no, not as such, but I'm a harpist.

C: Tough! *B, C and D snigger.*

D: People like you are never satisfied are you?

C: Too right. Sip your wine, sit on the blanket and enjoy yourself. *'A' sits resignedly but then gets up.*

B: Now what?

A: I thought I might have a game of football.

B: Football?

C: Absolutely not.

D: Despicable.

B: God definitely did not tell us to play football on day seven.

A: But He didn't tell us <u>not</u> to play football did He?

C: That is not the point.

A: I enjoy football.

D: That is well out of order.

C: Do you think we enjoy sitting on blankets all day long?

A: Football is relaxing.

B: I think we should write this down for everyone to remember, agreed? *C and D nod. B produces paper and pencil and writes.* Right, here we go. On the seventh day you shall sit on a blanket and sip wine.

D: Occasionally.

B: Yes, sip wine occasionally.

A: Is that what God means by resting... getting cramped, bored and frightened of our own shadows?

B: What else could the meaning be?

A: That's it, I've had enough! *He stands.*

B: Where are you going?

A: I'm off. If that is what it is all about then I am going to rest, relax and enjoy myself. *'A' walks off. B, C and D look at each other.*

B, C, and D: *together* Heathen!

Play the same sequence of God Shuffled His Feet as at the beginning.

Bread of Heaven

Characters:

Doctor Wither: cheerfully dismissive

Mr Jones: anxious

Scene: A surgery. Wither sits behind a desk, writing. Mrs Jones enters.

Jones: Morning Doctor Wither

Wither: Morning Mrs ... er ...

Jones: J –

Wither: No, don't tell me. Let me guess, I mean check. Ah yes, Mrs Bones.

Jones: Jones.

Wither: I meant Jones. Those Bs look just like Js sometimes don't they?

Jones: *laughing nervously.* Yes.

Wither: And how are you today? Not very well or you wouldn't be here would you? *laughs.* Now let me see. *He examines Mrs Jones in a cursory way.* Ah-ha!

Jones: Have you identified the problem?

Wither: Certainly. Tense, nervous headache? Stressed out? Suffering from road rage? You need Naffrin. *to audience* Naffrin reaches the parts other cures can't reach!

Jones: Well, I'm not sure. I think it's …

Wither: Unable to eat, unable to sleep, unable to stop.

Jones: Perhaps, but it's more like …

Wither: Fed up, lazy, boring, spotty.

Jones: No.

Wither: You need Naffrin!

Jones: Naffrin?

Wither: Nine out of ten cats prefer it. Ask a doctor.

Jones: I am not a cat.

Wither: Not assertive enough. *slaps Jones.*

Jones: Ow!

Wither: Do people ignore you? Next. Just a joke!

Jones: Definitely not, it's just …

Wither: Edgy, fretty, morbid? Full of energy. Drained of energy, desire, dread?

Jones: No, no, no! It is just that I am hungry.

Wither: Hungry? You mean food? Well eat!

Jones: No, not that sort of hunger.

Wither: Have some cheese.

Jones: Cheese?

Wither: Or cake, spaghetti, pilchards, poached eggs, soup; yams, ham, spam, lamb.

Jones: *grabbing Wither.* I don't mean that sort of hunger. I feel empty inside; not my stomach but my heart, my spirit. There is something missing in my life. I need something to live for, to know that this life is not the end. I don't want to leave everybody I love.

Wither: Oh, I see - that sort of hunger. I think I know what you need.

Jones: You do?

Wither: Yes, you need bread.

Jones: Bread?

Wither: Cob, farmhouse, wholemeal, granary, sourdough, rye, pita, croissant, brioche...

Jones: Stop it! *pause* You're right, I do need bread – some everlasting bread, some heavenly bread; a morsel to strengthen me; a crumb of comfort to fill this aching void inside me; to sweeten the bitter end. Is there no hope? No bread of heaven?

Wither: Bread of Heaven? Rubbish! I suggest you see a psychiatrist, or a Welshman. Now I really must get on. Next! *Jones leaves, sadly.* Bread of Heaven? Half-baked if you ask me.

Floccinaucinihilipilification

What is the longest word in the English language that is not a technical scientific term? It is not as you might think antidisestablishmentarianism. No, there is a word with one more letter namely, floccinaucinihilipilification, meaning the habit of regarding something as worthless. It is the schoolboy's delight.

As to it's usage we have all met people who display floccinaucinihilipilification I'm sure. They are the 'cup half empty' rather than 'cup half full' types. Whatever information, initiative or idea they receive they react negatively and soon weave it into a gloomy condemnation of all and sundry. In this context the f-word (as I shall call it) was used notably in the House of Commons by Jacob Rees-Mogg in 2012, to describe the lack of worthwhile activity demonstrated by members of the European Parliament.

The origin of the f-word is, like so many words, veiled in mists of rumour and speculation. One possible explanation is that pupils at Eton college (where else) strung together as many words as they could from their Latin grammar books whilst trying to retain a meaning in English, thus flocci (a wisp of wool) + nauci (a trifle) + nihil (nothing) + pilus (a hair – in the sense of a trifle or worthless) + fication (genitive verb form).

Another idea is that the word was invented by one William Shenstone, a friend of the writer Sir Walter Scott, and used in a letter to him in 1741.

Surely it is only a matter of time before someone displaces the f-word as the longest English word, merely by adding the prefix anti. You heard it here first, folks.

Hang on. I have just heard a rumour that the Oxford English Dictionary now includes supercalifragilisticexpialidocious. Well, my feelings towards that action could definitely be described as floccinaucinihilipilificatious!

(Note from editor: I thought the longest word was 'ultraantidisestablishmentarianism', but I suppose this would spoil the story.)

Me: Yes.

Idle Thoughts

Recently our writing group heard about lady who writes for Mills and Boon. Apparently, she didn't start writing until she retired and since then she has completed over fifty books of the romantic type. She writes according to a formula that Mills and Boon provide, with so many words, such and such a plot line and so on. It seems quite a lucrative idea; therefore I thought I would have a go

Like many writers in this genre the lady uses a pen name so I am using one. The way to get this is to take the name of your first pet then add on your mother's maiden name. This can produce some interesting results. Here is mine...

Argentine Tango by Tufty Woodcock

Fray Fantaroni swept her long black hair behind her ears and opened the diary. She reclined languorously on the chaise longue and prepared to read. Not without lingering regrets, however, because she had taken it from Facundo without him knowing. 'Oh, Facundo,' she breathed to herself. 'If only you knew what effect you have on me.'

Just the feel of the diary moved Fray with inexplicable longings. It was so smooth and shiny, so expensive and tasteful. She hugged it to herself and imagined it to be him, here beside her, on her. She remembered the first time they had met, in this poor yet beautiful and romantic outpost of Zanzibar, he an Argentinean diplomat with special responsibility for the Third World and she, a nurse with Medecins sans Frontieres. How cruel for him to be married, and yet how abandoned in her passion that knowledge made her feel, knowing that he would only be hers for a short time. That was why it was important for her to take his diary, she reasoned. She had to know more about this man who had swept her off her feet like a rough yet handsome gaucho throwing his bolas on her pampas. In her imagination he bestrode the bare estancias of her body, taking what he wanted, where he wanted, at heart a rough cow hand but with a silky and sophisticated exterior.

Fray could wait no longer. She had to know what he had thought of their first time, the time he had picked her like the feathery wand of a pampas grass and changed her universe forever. From here to eternity she would always have a little of the gaucho in her.

She ran her sensitive fingertips over the gold embossment on the front of the diary which read Facundo Valentin Bentos, and then furtively, nervously excited she turned to the day of their first meeting, the day when he had made sweet love to her. On reflection that was unusual, most people make a date first. A tiny cloud of doubt drifted into the blue sky of her happiness and threatened a little dampness. Surely he would recall the event with the same tenderness and affection as she. 'If only I could keep that tenderness,' she mused. 'If only he were not married then I would not have to be Fray Fantaroni; I could be Fray Bentos.'

Fray fretted with frustration. 'I know that first time wasn't ideal'. He had taken her across a table, the mad, impetuous fool. It was a shame they were now barred from that particular restaurant. How he had whispered sweet nothings as the moon rose over the bill on the table whilst the television in the corner relayed the cheer as David Beckham scored against Argentina.

'Goal,' ejaculated Facundo, with a dying fall in his voice.

'I must see what he thought about that volcanic and yet fragrant event,' agonised Fray.

And so she read, 'Monday - pissed off as Argentina lost to England; on the plus side, had sex with some tart.'

Peter Lancaster

From the pen of that colossus of the Mills and Boon world, a story of love, unrequited love, thwarted love and every other kind of love.

The Garden of Delights
by Tufty Woodcock

Rosemary Twine pushed her squeaky shopping trolley sulkily down the compost aisle of Eden Vale Yoghurt garden centre.

'Not many ideas for Christmas presents on this aisle', she grumbled; although there was that woman from the Rotary Club.

'I can't help it if her husband finds me attractive'. She had blurted it out loud.

Rosemary blushed and bit her full, bottom lip, an anxious expression momentarily clouding her dreamy, grey eyes. Then she laughed softly, shook her long red hair and whisked her trolley on towards the ornamental chippings section; squeak, squeak.

So far she had bought a miniature singing Christmas tree (a present for Mother), a large bunch of festive holly and a bumper box of crackers,

'But who to pull one with?' she giggled to herself. 'Well, there's Tom Veale, the butcher'. Tom Veale ran the pork butcher's shop on the high street. Rosemary always admired the way he handled his chopper before bringing it down on a joint of meat; and he was well off, the butcher's was a nice little business. She pursed her full lips, the bottom now bearing the faintest tooth marks.

Then there was Dick, the bin man, or 'waste disposal executive' as he liked to call himself. She always gave him a tip at Christmas (usually the tip was along the lines of 'make sure you wear thermals in winter').

Maybe Harry, the window cleaner; he always gave her a cheerful wink.

In her reverie Rosemary had cleared the chippings and was now idling past a row of flashing gnomes.

'Ooh, I fancy one of those', she cooed. 'They remind me of old Mr Turnbush, the gardener'.

'But is that what I really want for Christmas?' she asked herself. 'What about romance? What about the love and companionship of a good man?'

She brushed away a tear as the strains of 'Jingle Bells' struck up from a brass band over by the wassailing balls and walked swiftly on towards the tills, which were also jingling merrily.

Suddenly she was stopped in her tracks by the sight of a broad back crouching in front of her. The broad back was topped by tousled hair. Sweat glinted on bare arms, busy stacking shelves. Before she knew it Rosemary had inadvertently bumped her trolley into the well developed haunches beneath the back, the tousled hair and the bare arms. The holly made contact.

'Ow,' said a voice, and a face turned towards Rosemary. It had finely chiselled features, dark eyes, and fine teeth, now grimacing in pain.

'I'm so sorry', gushed Rosemary, 'my mind was elsewhere'.

'Jeepers Sheila, watch where you're going will ya? I was just rearranging my baubles'. The back, hair, haunches and face added a pair of long legs as the man stood up, rubbing himself. 'That's going to be a sore thing. I won't be waltzing Matilda for a while.'

'Did you feel a prick?'

'Well I felt a bit stupid'.

'You're not Australian by any chance are you?' asked Rosemary.

'Sure am, cobber. Bill's the name.' One rough, sun tanned hand reached out to shake, whilst the other expertly pulled back a tab on a can of Fosters.

'What are you looking for?' he asked

'A double entendre',

So he gave her one. And as the moon rose over the glass roof of the garden centre ... *(Note from the editor: You're fired; too many double entendres)*

Pisygod Wibbly-Wobbly

Have you taken a long, hard look in the mirror recently? That was the question I posed to myself the other day. It gets more difficult the older you get, I find. Long gone are the days when I had to blow my fringe out of my eyes. In fact, the whole fringe is long gone; the fringe, the crown, the forelock and most of my other locks. What remains has turned grey. It says in the Bible somewhere that God numbers the very hairs on our head. Well if that is so then all I can say is that some of us are making his job a lot easier for him; I don't know whether mine would make it to three figures these days.

Speaking of figures, that's another thing that seems to have disappeared; no, not so much disappeared as expanded. When clothes shopping I now have to be euphemised by the labels: a 'fuller figure' meaning fat; 'small and portly' meaning short and fat. Oh yes, that's yet another thing – small; I appear to be shrinking in height (possibly too in other ways that I won't go in to).

Then there are the teeth. What happened to my dashing, white smile that made the ladies swoon? I could have rivalled Errol Flynn or Ryan O'Neal when I was young. Nowadays my teeth are yellowing, painful and resting on a bed of swollen, red gums. When I smile I am more likely to make people back away in fear; in close up they are more reminiscent of a film set from Night of the Living Dead. I mentioned these concerns to my dentist (who is even older than I am) and he asked me whether I had considered having a whitening procedure. 'I had mine done' he enthused, flashing a set of whited sepulchres at me. 'And now I can't keep the women off me'. Hmm, I'm not sure about that; more likely to be the healthy state of his bank balance.

No, no it can't carry on. Something must be done before I fail to recognise my own reflection and retreat hissing into dark corners when folk approach me.

It just so happened that some time later I arranged to visit a friend who lives in Colwyn Bay. One thing that Colwyn Bay has that our neck of the woods doesn't is the sea. And what can the sea be used for by those seeking fitness and health? Swimming for one thing. Bear in mind that I had been brooding about my appearance since the great mirror debacle (a study in pink, yellow and red) as outlined above.

My friend was frankly sceptical. 'It's a bad year for Weaver Fish', he said, helping himself to another rasher of bacon at breakfast. They eject spines full of poison if you tread on them; the most painful experience known to man apparently; guaranteed to reduce the strongest to a gibbering wreck. Then there are sharks; they've been spotted inshore this year. Oh, and watch where you are treading; there are razor sharp rocks just beneath the surface of the water in the bay. Our neighbour got cut to pieces the other week'. (This whilst lathering butter onto toast).

Nevertheless, I remained determined to get fit and swimming seemed a good a way as any to me. I borrowed some voluminous shorts from my scoffing (in both senses) friend and left him muttering darkly about the dangers of rag-worms and rip-tides.

Down on the beach I was suddenly transported back half a century: there was the pier, in all its Victorian, cast iron splendour; there were the seagulls, wheeling, wailing and pooping in equal measure. There was the sand, soft and warm between my toes, with the occasional sharp stone to make you double up in agony, ruining your macho parade down to the shoreline. There was the smell of ozone, the sound of the waves and of happy children making sandcastles; no swimmers though, a dark little cloud formed in the back of my mind and began to rain, wetly. With a perfect example of pathetic fallacy the dark little cloud was matched by one in the sky which made me shiver as I began to bare my manly torso.

Changing on the beach, or rather awkwardness about changing on the beach, is a peculiarly British phenomenon. Many a time I have attempted to cover my white body with a towel whilst removing swimming trunks and then engaged in the fiendishly difficult task of putting on underpants over wet, sandy feet, without success. How can it be that something designed to go over your feet, ie underwear, becomes so unbiddable and wayward when wet? I remember in Portugal trying to do just such a thing as the bronzed Portuguese around me bared all, towelling their dangling bits with gay abandon.

Anyway, I eventually was transformed, and casting towel aside strode palely to the beckoning sea. Still there were no other bathers. I dipped my toe in the old briny and tried not to flinch and immediately withdraw it. 'Bracing,' I announced to anyone within earshot.

The colour of the sea was a greeny-brown, and very murky. I couldn't make out any Weaver fish, rag worms or sharks, and no rip tide seemed to be about to drag me out away from the shore, so I persisted. There comes a moment particularly delicate for a gentleman when the water starts to lap around his nether regions; best to get straight in from here so I dived rather grandiosely into the breaking surf (no-one can hear you shrieking underwater).

Soon I had got used to the cold. 'This is the life', I thought, having survived the initial shock.

Speaking of shocks, although the water had the consistency of pea and ham soup, you could just make out one or two larger bodies beneath the surface. One was a rock, best avoided; one was a lump of seaweed (no trouble) and a third looked wobbly and translucent, with waving fronds or tendrils underneath it. Surely it couldn't be a jellyfish could it? My friend hadn't warned me about jellyfish. At that very moment somebody threw an electric toaster into the water (or it felt like it) and sharp stabbing pulses of pain began to run up and down my body. Have you ever splashed yourself with hot fat or received a jolt from a car battery? It was a bit like that, except it didn't stop.

With what little strength I had remaining I turned for shore and sort of swam/dragged/moaned/grieved into the shallows. A small group of curious onlookers, who had been observing my antics for some time, finally thought the spectacle worth raising their heads from a sunbathing declination. 'Are you alright mate?'

asked one in a disinterested sort of way. 'Perfectly, thank you, not a problem,' I lied. My body was beginning to throb and swell in a somewhat alien way, as though I were turning into the Thing, or as if partly cooked popcorn was just beginning to puff and pop in the oven.

It was the first time I had been stung by a jellyfish (for that was indeed what had happened to me) and the sensation of being electrocuted didn't leave me for twenty-four hours. The pharmacist sucked his teeth and shook his head. 'Could be anything,' he said vaguely, and waved a jar of cream in front of me. 'Come back if it hasn't stopped in a week'. A week!

My friend was still eating when I returned from my fitness spree. 'Hmmm, you don't look so good' he remarked objectively. 'Ah well, better luck next time. Would you like some of this delicious spiced apple jelly?'

Oh yes, and are you wondering about pisygod wibblywobbly? Well, it's cod welsh for jellyfish. Get it? Cod welsh.

Peter Lancaster

The Missing Link

'How much is this one?'

The short, squat man had been looking at the painting for some time. The proprietor had watched him as he circled the gallery, his eyes never still, examining each picture in turn: the artist's signatures, the palette of colours used, the composition and the subject matter. But always he returned to this particular painting.

The man was about sixty years old, with thin, greying hair and thick spectacles (through which his darting eyes were magnified. He was overweight, although not obese, and wore a black polo shirt over black slacks. 'Presumably to look slimmer', thought the proprietor. 'He knows something about art but I reckon there's still a profit to be made out of him'.

'Do you mean the one by Aleph Bet? Six-thousand pounds'

The short, squat man pursed his lips and shook his head slightly. As he did so a faint sheen of sweat was visible on his forehead, illuminated by the ceiling lights in the gallery. His expression conveyed incredulity.

'Six,' he echoed. 'What's it called?'

'The Missing Link', said the proprietor.

The picture showed a night sky with stars and moon, over the silhouettes of a range of mountains, with a dusty plain in the foreground. Mist hung round the valleys of the mountains and the moon cast strange shadows on them so that the eye played tricks, seeing shapes of things that were not there.

'Or perhaps they are', muttered the man to himself. He fancied he could see human faces in scree fields, human shoulders and backs in the outlines of ridges and valleys; dark arms entwining themselves in moments of agony or ecstasy.

Somewhere in the middle of the plain a large boulder, resembling a shambling ape-like figure, looked to be staring at the moon, its back to the viewer.

'Can you get it off the wall for me please so I can have a closer look?'

The proprietor obliged reluctantly, lifting the cord off the hook at the back of the painting and carefully manhandling the not inconsiderable frame onto the gallery counter. 'Was this guy serious?' People generally were content to view paintings on the wall.

As if he had been reading his thoughts the short, squat man said, 'It makes it much easier to examine the paint.' He thrust his large hand into a pocket in his black slacks and produced a jeweller's loupe, with which he proceeded to examine the painting in detail.

'Used a mixture of corn starch, food colouring and a binding agent, to create the dust,' he said, almost to himself.

The proprietor was quite impressed; he was an ordinary shop owner; he had not known how the painting had been created. Frankly he was bored with the painting - with all paintings actually, and with the gallery. It was a dark, sterile place, away from fresh air and the garden at his house. That was his real passion these days. He loved to plant things and watch them grow; to till the earth and harvest the fruit in season. He smiled to himself at the thought. Selling paintings was only a means to an end.

The man was looking at the back of the painting now. The proprietor could see his own label, 'Adam's Gallery', stuck to it, revealed for the first time in a long time.

The man placed the painting the right way up on the counter and turned smiling to the proprietor. 'Well, Adam,' he said in a leading sort of way. He seemed taller and broader than before, and the eyes had stopped jumping around; they were looking in a measured way at the proprietor, keen but not unkindly.

'You want six-thousand pounds for this painting? You want a lot. How about I give you seven?'

'Seven?' the proprietor blinked in surprise. 'But that's more than I'm asking.'

'It's in my gift Adam,' said the man. 'You see I am Aleph Bet the artist. I created this painting and seven is the right number for it, and for you.'

Visitors to Adam's Gallery later that day were disappointed not to find the proprietor in attendance. The place was open, the lights and heating were on and valuable paintings were still on the walls - there for the taking by the unscrupulous. All was the same except for one painting. 'The Missing Link' had changed, almost out of recognition. The night sky was giving way to a spectacular sunrise which dispelled the darkness and disorder of the shadows. The ridges of the mountains sparkled like diamonds in the dawn light; the plain could be seen to contain not dust but myriads of plants, shrubs, trees and flowers. Most significantly, the ape-like boulder was now revealed as the figure of an ordinary man, tending the ground.

One more thing had changed. Under the signature Aleph Bet someone had added, apparently in the same hand, 'I am who I am'.

Peter Lancaster

Fall

I used to revile the American phrase for autumn: 'The Fall', but nowadays I quite like it's evocation of the spent summer, the fall into quietude and gentle sleep.

During 'The Fall' this year the phrase on everybody's lips is 'Supermoon'. This means a moon larger than normal, when it comes closest to the Earth on its endless orbit round our planet. A supermoon exerts such immense gravitational forces that the Earth is squeezed, like an orange in the hand of a cocktail maker. There is to be one tonight and in addition, there is to be a red moon in the early hours of the morning due to an eclipse, so rare that another will not be seen for thirty-three years.

After our evening meal my wife and I wander down the lane to the park, where there are no street lights or buildings to obscure the night sky. It is a warm, still, late-September night, and as we lean on the farm gate to look we see, hanging low in the eastern sky, our supermoon, like a mature cheddar cheese. It is definitely full, and bigger than normal, and it is just beautiful, sailing majestically over the hills, like an old friend, returned from exotic foreign parts to regale us with tales of the unexpected; thrilling, yet safe and comforting. It is not red yet; that is forecast for later.

Whether it is the moon, the mild, wood-smoke scented evening or the quietude, but suddenly I am whisked back more than half a century to bonfire nights of my childhood. I vividly recall the excitement and anticipation of the big event, collecting fireworks of weird and wonderful appearance, with names such as 'Roman Candle', 'Catherine Wheel', or 'Rip-Rap'. (We were protected from the knowledge that the names might have sprung from something unpleasant).

There was the joy of walking along the road in the dark to the field at the end, clutching our tins of fireworks, wrapped up against the cold. We were not normally allowed outside after dark and this gave us a thrill of conspiracy. There was the bonfire we had been collecting wood for, for weeks, looking impossibly high and dangerously combustible. There was poor Guy on the top with his pillow body, stuffed stockings for limbs and a face mask. It was bad news for Catholics. Guy had been paraded around the neighbourhood on a go-kart as a means of getting pennies to buy fireworks.

Our dads lit the fire and supervised the letting off of fireworks. It was only as teenagers that we started putting fireworks in places they were not meant to go: rip-raps behind girls, bangers in letterboxes, rockets launched on dangerous trajectories. As younger ones we just enjoyed the simple, innocent pleasures of toffee apples, parkin and burnt jacket potatoes.

And I reflect that it is the supermoon that has made me fall into this reverie; or rather not fall but with backward mutterings of dissevering power has made me a child again, just for a moment.

Peter Lancaster

The White Lie

'So I've been told', she said,
'The rainbow doesn't have a pot of gold,
But light refracting art;
A colour beauty accident,
Not 'Act of God', intelligent design.
This universe is strung along by chance,
Not talk of 'meant to be'.
Your feelings simply chemically formed.
Don't look askance'.

She languorously spread
A hand upon the bed we had unmade,
Unravelled like a Catherine Wheel
Of fiery red, electric blue.
Now hers the heat, desire, lust,
And mine the love a white lie lost.

Idle Thoughts

These final two pieces, The White Rose and Keep Faith, are reflections on the sacrifice of some brave people who gave their lives standing up for what they believed in.

The White Rose was a loose affiliation or secret society of certain professors and students at Munich University during the 1930s and 1940s. Its purpose was to oppose the Nazis through intellectual debate and by leafleting the campus to try and gain support for their cause. They were eventually betrayed, arrested and ritually beheaded by the Gestapo, in 1943.

Maximillian Kolbe was a Polish priest who died as a prisoner in Auschwitz, in 1941, because he offered himself as a substitute for execution. A Jewish inmate had escaped from the Concentration Camp and as a reprisal the Nazis chose ten prisoners to be shot. One of those chosen, Franciszek Gajowniczek, wept that he would never see his wife and family again, and so Kolbe put himself forward to take his place. His offer was accepted...

The White Rose

Interrogated faces,
White with tension under lights,
Thrown in relief on concrete,
Petals of a dying rose.

Peter Lancaster

Keep Faith ©

Whatever happened * To the Man-God * Christ * Messiah Jesus * Down the line * Two thousand years? * Things didn't go too well for Him * Did they? * A failed Jew * Some said. * Not much of a god * To let them *

Spit * In his face. * Nails * Hammered * Through wrists * Tortured * To death. * His ending * Pain * And loss ** He suffered all * The randomness of life. * Down * In the filth * And broken glass * The spittle * And the blood -flecked froth * Of the world * Writhing and agonising. * Better * Curse God * And die. ** Ten thousand angels * At his command * Might have * swooped * Down from heaven * With a mighty * Beating * Of wings and * Rescued * Him; *

Carried Him off * To a better place * No more to think * On bad mankind. ** But H e chose to stay * At His torture post. * Chose * To swallow all the pain and wrong * Chose * My shabbiness and yours * The lack of * Care * Or love * The cruelty * Poverty * Sneer * Leer * The maiming * And all the casual acts * Of a fallen world * He took upon Himself * Jesus * The Man-God * So that with His * Bloodied hand * He could reach down and * Pull us * Up to God * See Him * Face to face. ** As He chose, * So I choose Him. * Keep faith. **